THINKING ABOUT WOMEN

Thinking About Women

MARY ELLMANN

A HARVEST BOOK

Harcourt Brace Jovanovich, Inc., New York

In memory of Nora Donahue

Contents

Preface: An Interview

The general nature of this book was discussed in an interview conducted, several months ago, at the National Institute of Interviews, Lake Norman, N. M. It seems convenient now to reproduce the exchange as a reader's guide to all that follows. It also seems convenient to abbreviate Interviewer and my name as I and ME.

M.E.

I. Do you need any particular environment in which to work?

ME. I like a room without a view, preferably a closet. Oddly enough, I've never worked in the attic. The front of our attic has a view, you see, and then the back part is jammed with old toys.

I. Do you need seclusion?

ME. I wish I could say I'd been locked in a room. It's pedestrian not to have a tyrannical husband. My work is, in this way, deprived of pathetic circumstance.

I. Never mind, perhaps you have a writer's costume.

ME. Only a navy blue woollen bathrobe. An effortlessly drab garment, I hate answering the phone in it. But I just don't have any faded dungarees or open-necked sport shirts. They're for men.

I. They're for men?

ME. They're for men.

I. I see. Well, speaking of men, could you explain why you are writing about women?

ME.   I didn't want to overreach. Right from the start I thought: ME, you must limit yourself to *half* of the human race.

I.   Then you were not prompted by feminism?

ME.   Please.

I.   Oh. Feminism is out, isn't it?

ME.   Well, yes, in the way principles all go out before they're practiced. Say a bride gets locked in the bathroom. The guests have gone home from the wedding, they've already forgotten their sanction of this event —which, as it happens, hasn't quite happened. Still, people can't go on throwing rice forever.

I.   But think of the poor bride.

ME.   It's better for her to gnaw at the door than to argue in the mirror about her right to get out.

I.   Then you do not have a female program of your own?

ME.   You phrase things peculiarly.

I.   I scarcely know what word will not offend you. I will try again. You don't have a program for women?

ME.   No. No program.

I.   Ah! But perhaps you will define the attitude of the woman toward the gun, the ship and the helicopter?

ME.   Impossible.

I.   It's been done. A man has done it for men.

ME.   Indeed.

I.   Then have you something to contribute to our knowledge of human sexual responses?

ME.   You mean with wires and thermometers and all.

I.   Yes.

ME. No.

I.   This is fun, isn't it? Now tell me, is your work con-
     cerned with the status of American women?

ME. You make everything sound like a symposium.

I.   Forgive me once again. Nonetheless, a good deal of
     work has been done on this subject. And it looks as
     though their status is slipping.

ME. I applaud this work. I deplore this slipping.

I.   But have you studied the statistics on it?

ME. You touch on a personal matter which I am of course
     willing to reveal to the public. My internist has asked
     me to cut down gradually on my consumption of sta-
     tistics about American women.

I.   Why?

ME. It's sort of sad. Say I read that only nineteen Ameri-
     can women became orthodontists in 1962. I am hu-
     miliated, depressed. I cry easily. It's days before I
     think to be glad that so few *wanted* to be orthodon-
     tists, do you see?

I.   I think so. You like only statistics of success.

ME. Perhaps. But I think it's worse than that. I am af-
     flicted by miscomprehension, the failures often seem
     to me successes. For example, we know exactly how
     many American women interrupted their husbands'
     anecdotes at dinner parties in 1966. Quite a few,
     as a matter of fact—204,648 wives. But of course
     just to *count* them is to say they have failed at the
     table. This complicated thing, interruption, is made
     quite simply bad. And yet all dialogue, like you and

me, might be defined as the prevention of monologue. And think of the other guests—how can we hope that they wanted to hear the husbands out? Perhaps these wives are socialists who place the liveliness of the party before their own favor with their husbands.

I.   I think perhaps you might say *Yes* or *No* for a while again.

ME.   Or think of the official successes. I am afraid of the ideal unions toward which counselors propel us. You take an intolerable man and an intolerable woman and put them in an apartment together, and then if they are both *mature*, and each tries to *understand* the other's monstrous nature, a *good marriage* results.

I.   It cannot be wrong to urge understanding.

ME.   No, it must be right in social work. But in novels, say, misunderstanding reasserts itself. Its resilience is apparent, and one feels a grudging admiration for resilience, the admiration one might feel for a viral strain which all the aspirin in the world won't eradicate.

I.   Then really, you relish confusion—or even sore throats.

ME.   I said it was a grudging admiration. There's an enormous number of opinions about women, and I will admit I'm impressed by the regularity and the intensity with which they are expressed. Some are more plausible than others, but their plausibility or implausibility isn't so much the point. It's their *reiteration*.

I.   Perhaps an example.

ME.   With pleasure. In the novel *The Awakening* by Kate

Chopin, the woman is annoyed when the man says he won't fan himself because when you stop fanning you're hotter than if you never fanned at all. That sounds like Tennyson, doesn't it? But whether the man is saying something true or not doesn't much matter. It is a tiresome thing to say which some people feel they *must* say. People also say things like *Women have a natural capacity for self-sacrifice* or *Women feel deeply*. Either statement is possibly true, certainly tedious, and evidently irresistible.

I. Now I think *I'll* cry. I never knew women suffered from such compliments, that they were tormented by praise.

ME. You know, a funny thing, you look like a tape recorder yourself. I'll bet you're married to a walkie-talkie.

I. Women always get personal. If you disagree with them, they insult your wife.

ME. If I were willing to play that game, which I certainly am not, I'd say men always get *im*personal. If you hurt their feelings, they make Boyle's Law out of it.

I. Surely we have both benefited from Boyle's Law?

ME. Which one is it?

I. A busy little person like you can look it up for herself.

ME. Dear me. Let's us be abstract again, shall we?

I. I never wanted to be anything else.

ME. Then think a thought now.

I. Very well. It has crossed my mind that there are just as many opinions about men.

ME. Those are central opinions, about Humanity or Mankind. Opinions about women are about an eccentric phenomenon, which is felt to exert some obscure influence upon the center. Like the moon, which is always female, on the tides. Or on dogs, disturbing the dogs' peace of mind.

I.   But then perhaps you'll simply confess that men are more curious than women.

ME.   That is a possibility men often raise. And perhaps they're right. Historically, at any rate, there's perhaps some correlation between authority and curiosity. As soon as something is controlled, it becomes a problem or a puzzle to the one who controls it. We're all uncomfortably aware of the prurience with which the white racist speculates about the Negro. Or say a mayor in Milwaukee imposes a curfew. Then he can't stand not knowing what all those people who are forbidden to come out, are doing in their houses. It's the way the most powerful governments, like our own, seem to have the most spies. But I don't know why I put it so unpleasantly. Actually, this curiosity must be redemptive. It suggests the one still wants a connection with the other.

I.   I trust you are not saying that all men are mayors of Milwaukee.

ME.   You're still pouting, aren't you? It was only a metaphor.

I.   I got the distinct impression—

ME.   Nonsense. At least nonsense here—or say in England or Sweden. Lots of American men say American men don't feel like American men any more. And I'm not trying to speak of other places. I wouldn't dare. What could I say about men and women in India? Food has all the authority in starvation. Sexual politics and sexual opinions, and I suppose sexuality itself, are all fringe benefits of eating.

I. But in the United States, let's say, you would like to put an end to tedious opinions about women?

ME. I'm not sure. Imagine the tedium *without* them! Anyway, they're not simply tedious. They're often bold— I mean in their flights beyond embarrassment. I rather like their crazy proliferation too—in that sense, sexual opinions are sexual themselves. They mate with each other and multiply—incessantly! Also, the little ones look like the big ones. I've come to like watching them bob in and out of books—novels, especially. Like those goldfish that go endlessly in and out of their grottoes.

I. Tell me, do you often think about fish and tides?

ME. Connect my crabbed little mind with water now, flowing streams and all that. Go ahead. Do me a Molly Bloom. I dare you.

I. I have neither the time nor the desire to study your mind. I shall only say that you pretend more detachment than I believe you feel.

ME. Perhaps. But since I am most interested in women as *words*—as the words they pull out of mouths, I am not pretending to *some* detachment, some is real.

I. And the rest?

ME. What can I say? [*A Gallic gesture here.*] One can imagine an impossibly different world, in which this kind of attention was diverted from women to some other phenomenon. They might like that. A suspension of *belief*, for a change. Or eight sexes instead of two —that would divide all available attention by four.

I. By seven, I think.

ME. We are discussing close attention, I, not short division.

I. But close attention is a compliment, isn't it?

ME. Compliments again! But what if fixed attention and critical attention are the same? Like those love poems where the beloved's ugly hands or crooked teeth turn up in the second stanza. Of course she is presumably loved the more for her defect—but still, there are those damn teeth. Nothing can be looked at very long, that's why lovers fall asleep. And then so much attention is unloving all over. I am thinking of the kind of attention the English newspapers focus on the United States. Or the way people at the zoo stare at cobras or at the outrageous backsides of baboons.

I. We have come a long way now from the topic of women.

ME. On the contrary. We are just beginning it.

❧ I ❧

SEXUAL ANALOGY

◈ In exhaustion or illness, or shortly after sexual intercourse, each person approaches that point of detachment in which human sexuality appears in its essential simplicity and multiplicity—the two forms and the one union between them, repeated in every time and place of human life. But this is an apparition which the slightest encounter with another person, or even the thought of such an encounter, or only a revivified sense of the person's own body by itself, immediately erases. Detachment is gone, and involvement so thorough that one is ordinarily no more conscious of the monotony of sex than he is conscious, in breathing, of the monotony of air.

Men are stronger than women, and the reproductive role of women is more prolonged and more arduous than that of men. An utterly practical (though not an ideal) society would be one in which these facts were of such importance that all men and women were totally absorbed in their demonstration—that is, in the use of strength and the completion of pregnancies. Both sexes would live without intermissions in which to recognize their own monotony or, more often, to describe the complex fascination in which their senses disguised it. In the past, there have been Egyptian desert tribes in which the men fought constantly and the women constantly replenished the army through childbirth. This is perhaps as close as human beings, in an extreme economy of war, can come to unthinking life. Yet even in such a tribe, sexual analogy would exist. If a wounded tribesman lying on the ground watched a large, round cloud cross the sky, he would die thinking, That cloud is pregnant.

But leisure is primarily mindful, and as we escape the exigency of sexual roles, we more fully indulge the avocation of sexual analogies. The proportions of the two seem particularly grotesque now when the roles themselves have taken on an unprecedented irrelevance. It is strangely as though we had come upon circumstances which render the physiology of sex nearly superfluous, and therefore comic in its eager and generous self-display. This element of excess is marked of course in all sexual systems; it has only become ridiculous for human beings, if not for hollyhocks and salmon, as the demands upon the supply have diminished. Society need no longer encourage conception and pregnancy; on the contrary, it is obliged in general to discourage both. Both increasingly depend upon a personal choice, which society merely condones. In fact, it does not even condone the choice unless the woman is privately supported. In Waukegan, Illinois, it has been proposed that unmarried pregnant poor women be sent to jail, and few human beings have been less welcomed into existence than the illegitimate children of these women. Only the blind and intent egotism of infancy protects them from dismissal. (Society: You are

3

still another too many. Infant: I will breathe nonetheless.)
The reproductive capacity of women, then, has become socially gratuitous, obsolescent. It seems most markedly so
among the poor, only because money shields this aspect of
the body as it does all other aspects—at the same time that
it provides access to means of its control. But it is impossible
now for any people, outside of novels and the Catholic
Church, to strike heroic genitive postures. The rest recognize a period in which birth control is essential if they are
not to end fighting each other for space or eating each other,
as in a world-wide Stalingrad under siege, for food.

Similarly, the physical strength of men has become gratuitous. It has to be maintained now for its own sake; its de-
generation is as debilitating as its maintenance is futile. So,
the epoch of exercise, the expenditure of energy for the sake
of expenditure—as women sometimes shop for the sake of
shopping. The chief remaining function of strength, like
that of reproduction, is personal gratification. There are still
states of entertainment and of excitement in which strength
is coveted: in swimming, for example, and perhaps in at-
tracting (or overpowering) women. But nothing lives apart
from other things, and it is clear now that even in esthetic
(in the sense of attractive) terms, strength is not conse-
quential. It is as though, useless, strength could no longer
be liked. Apparently, there is more point now in advertising
shirts on one-eyed or one-armed models than on men who
have not achieved some intriguing deformity. As in the
novel, the selection of a hero (an obsolescent term as well)

4

bypasses all Olympic chances to settle, somewhat desperately, upon dwarfs and demigoats.

Conventional social scientists, of course, continue to study the male psyche in terms of physical strength. The Canadian psychiatrist, Karl Stern, in his *Flight from Woman*, recalls its past services: tunneling through mountains and building slag heaps and cutting down trees. He notices, with the customary regret, that most of these services are now outmoded (there aren't enough trees left, after all, and slag heaps slide down onto schools), but he is eager to indicate other ways in which the strength might still be manifested. He has proposed the ineluctable basement workshop where at the end of the school-and-office day children might see their fathers driving nails and sawing logs. Dr. Stern also finds the old outdoor energies of the male reallocated to the space capsule. But this of course, as an equivalent of settling the West, is even less plausible than Sunday carpentry. The space program, on the contrary, indicates the weak way we must live now. It's not only that the female body, as Valentina Tereshkova so charmingly demonstrated, is equally capable of the quasi-exertions of space. It's rather that the whole character of that activity is *in*activity; it marks like tranquillizers the advance of a period in which we will have to value passivity, as we have valued aggression in the past, or not be able to value ourselves.

The shape of the rocket no doubt misleads many observers, along the cement paths of Freudian correspondences, to a masculine conception of the program. But its human

5

role is not energetic or forceful. The astronaut's body is as awkward and encumbered in the space suit as the body of a pregnant woman. It moves about with even more graceless difficulty. And being shot up into the air suggests submission too, rather than enterprise. Like a woman being carted to a delivery room, the astronaut must sit (or lie) still, and go where he is sent. Even the nerve, the genuine courage it takes simply not to run away, is much the same in both situations —to say nothing of the shared sense of having gone too far to be able to change one's mind.

It is, then, a time in which sexual differences are more visual than actual. We *see* a man doing what we would ordinarily think of as feminine, sitting still, and manage to think of it as masculine because a man is doing it. Some people manage even to continue to think of men standing up when in fact they are sitting down. It is possible that we will all proceed to live in just such a mode of contradiction, with no more effect than a gradually mounting sense of our own incredibility. Perhaps as long as sexual interest in any sense is strong, we will continue to comprehend all phenomena, however shifting, in terms of our original and simple sexual differences; and to classify almost all experiences by means of sexual analogy. The persistence of the habit is even, conceivably, admirable. It might be taken as proof of the fertility of the human mind that, given so little sexual evidence, it should contrive so large a body of dependent sexual opinion. In our habits of sexual thought, the relation of evidence to analogy is like the relation of the female termite's tiny pinhead to the enormous belly from which she produces six thousand eggs a day. (A sexual analogy to the prevalence of sexual analogy.)

All that impairs the impression of prowess is the impression of doom. One could wish that sexual speculation, like the termite's fecundity, did not seem quite so involuntary and invariable. It is unpleasant, for example, to be *obliged* to divide the contents of the universe into the two categories of male and female. Particularly since Freud, we have come to know that we are less ingenious than slavish in our attribution of every extrorse form to the male and of every declivity to the female. It is as though this unending process of reduction by sexual analogy had been carried on, like the reduction of food to feces, at least inconspicuously before Freud, conspicuously since him. There is no evidence of Freud's having been dismayed by the process: he had the satisfaction of fixing it as an inescapable motion of the mind, and also of finding a use for it—as one fantastic key to real psychic preoccupations.

Much, however, of Freud's pragmatic enthusiasm has since been succeeded by impatience,* if not depression. What he revealed was not, of course, intended to be winning: his own intelligence, like Pope's, exposed a universal dullness, a Dunciad. One thinks now of Freud's (personal) and Jung's (collective) theories of the unconscious as dual confirmations of an innate human tedium. The first always suggests a relentless, stubborn and brutish force, capable at

* At the present time, for example, a person who points out breasts, thighs *et al.* in the contours of a landscape, is asked to leave the average car.

most of a mean craft, an obfuscation of experience, seizing upon elements of external reality to create confused and distorted statements of its narrow and repetitive needs. The second seems relatively lax and floating, will-less in tone, but the two are alike in at once codifying and pervading our modern sense of reiteration—of habits, rather than surprises, of the mind. It is impossible to wish the retraction of any knowledge; but if it were possible, one might wish not to have comprehended the involuntary workings of thought. Yet since this comprehension has therapeutic value, psychiatrists are properly honored in our society: they immerse themselves, for the sake of their patients, in a monotony more consistent than any formulated before Freud. Indeed they might drown in it, were it not for their own exertions: the secondary monotony of analytic commentary, laborious explanation piled upon effortless association. Nothing is more understandable, in this context, than Alain Robbe-Grillet's retaliative determination to describe even a banana grove without permitting the slightest human analogy to intrude. Perhaps a new tedium succeeds the old in his *Jealousy*, but it is a quixotic tedium—a heroic refusal, for once, to translate inhuman variety into terms of only men and women.

Ordinarily, not only sexual terms but sexual opinions are imposed upon the external world. All forms are subsumed by our concepts of male and female temperaments. Yeats's silver arrows pierce red hounds. The hunter is always male, the prey female. It is impossible not to see the plumage of the male bird as gay and cavalier, the subdued colors of the female as an airborne equivalent of the housedress. And yet, in fact, the plumage of the male is part of the natural importance of catching the eye of the inattentive female. Failure here could be catastrophic: if the female robin is not blinded by the redness of the male, there is evidently nothing to prevent her flying off with an oriole instead. So all butterflies are taken to be frivolous and effeminate creatures (social butterflies), though in mating seasons male butterflies, like rams, make a show of hostile and competitive virility. This goes unnoticed, I suppose, because butterflies fight with their wings, and until winged creatures are large and conspicuously fierce, eagles or buzzards, we tend to think of them all as female. All shrews too, like all butterflies, are females, though for less pretty reasons. At first associated with malign influence, as women too have been in many primitive cultures, the shrew's defect was gradually narrowed, in its application to women, to the afflictive habit of scolding. And yet, playing the same game, one would think it more plausible to consider the shrew feminine in its tendency to drop dead of fright during thunderstorms. Similarly, perhaps thanks to Melville, all whales are more or less males simply because they are big enough to scare men.* Whatever may

* All imagined forms of fear and punishment, like God and the Devil, are masculine. So are those aggressive powers, the sun and the wind, with the exception of American hurricanes. A keen sense of the *domestic* chaos brought about by hurricanes has recently led to their being named for women. One supposes that the moon will remain feminine ("the new moon with the old moon in her arms") until it is colonized by Russia

be the immense capacity of the female whale for that total dedication (frequently observed in female *persons*) to maternal and connubial tasks, goes unconsidered. The incomparable eccentricities of nature are obscured by sexual predisposition, and most often abused as well. The cow* and the sow are insulted with the woman (Joyce's Ireland is the old sow that eats her farrow), the mouse and the rat with the man, the cat with the woman, the dog with the man—the last, though, with the prominent exception of the bitch.

Like those of the external world, the intricacies of human beings are also understood in the exclusive terms of sexual physiology. This intellectual tyranny affects all relationships: we would perhaps be unconscious of its pervasive presence, if we were not conscious of slight fluctuations in its severity. To some extent, heterosexuals see members of their own sex (and homosexuals members of the opposite sex) without sexual bias. Most adults are also able to see small children as tiny, perfect abstractions of male and female reality.

---

or the United States (by bears or eagles). Only steady rain, an admitted sexual depressant, is neuter (The rain, *it* raineth all the day), though there are, of course, predictable sexual plays upon intermittent showers.

* One of the most puzzling remarks in Jung's "Psychological Aspects of the Mother Archetype" is that the *hare*, like the cow, has maternal associations. One can only conclude that German hares behave better than English hares, which are always thought of as intensely, even insanely, masculine—as in "mad as a March [the breeding season] hare."

Indeed, much of the affective power of children lies in our comprehending and admiring their sexual forms, without desire. Yet even the degree of intellectual freedom with which each sex may contemplate itself is impaired by chauvinism, the inescapable inclination of each genital system to consider its differences superiorities. And between the sexes, both the lowest submission to sexual consideration (incest) and the highest (and yet still partial) freedom from it occur within the family—in the relations of parents and children, brothers and sisters. But even this freedom, at its most humane, seems only to refine sexual consideration, substituting concern and affection for emulation and antagonism:

> It is written. A daughter is a vain treasure to her father. From anxiety about her he does not sleep at night; during her early years lest she be seduced, in her adolescence lest she go astray, in her marriageable years lest she does not find a husband, when she is married lest she be childless, and when she is old lest she practice witchcraft.*

In all those sexual interchanges which are neither personal nor affectionate, the reasoning is pseudoscientific: the impulse is to prefer rather than to define differences, and to classify by means of association. Only the digestive system, which is shared by the sexes, is not often sexually characterized. And recently Norman Mailer has tried, in his "Metaphysics of the Belly," to pre-empt even the large intestine as an aspect of a masculine ethic. Diseases too are presumably mutual misfortunes and therefore exempt from sexual judg-

* *Talmud* (Ben Sira. Sanhedrin 100 *b*).

11

ment. But actually, we think repeatedly in terms of disorders, like hair styles, which befit the sex. There is not just the punitive assignment of cancer of the uterus to the old virgin, like Auden's Miss Gee. The novel is rare now in which any woman is allowed to be stricken by an illness which is *not* connected with the sexual system. In retrospect, the discreet phthisis of earlier heroines seems innovative, and it is perhaps another mark of Flaubert's superiority that he allowed Emma Bovary to die of poisoning rather than of puerperal fever.

In health, however, the most popular route of association is that between the female reproductive organs and the female mind. This association is usually marked by large, simple conceptions, more noticeable for their tenacity than for their detail. It is, in fact, an ancient association: the Greek *hystera*, or womb, is the root of *hysteria* because it was believed that the mental disorder, to which women were particularly subject (and small wonder, with such medical attendants), was caused by disorders of the womb. We have now made so much progress that a woman may be hysterical without being subjected to a hysterectomy—though one should notice that the hysterectomy remains a favorite among factitious operations. (Still, with a middle-aged woman patient, when the surgeon thinks, What should I take out? the word *uterus* darts through his mind first.) The same fixed mode of thought runs uninterruptedly beneath the seeming expansion of our modern intellectual opinions. For example, when Bruno Bettelheim characterizes the male mind as *expansive* and *exploratory* and the female mind as *interiorizing*, it is ludicrously clear that he envisages a mental copulation between the two.* So too when Louis Auchincloss characterizes several American women novelists as *conservers* or *caretakers*. And when Norman Mailer pronounces that "Temples are for women." The female mind is repeatedly seen as an enclosed space in which what other and (as we always say) *seminal* minds have provided is stored away or tended or worshipped.

When the uterus-mind is seen as conservative or nutritive, it is praised. When it is seen as claustrophobic, it is blamed. By sexual correlation, all energy or enterprise is customarily assigned to male thought, and simple, accretive expectation to female thought. The one breaks through, the other broods. An immobility is attributed to the entire female constitution by analogy with the supposed immobility of the ovum. This imaginative vision of the ovum, like a pop art fried-egg-on-a-plate, is dependent of course upon a happy physiological vagueness. In actuality, each month the ovum undertakes an extraordinary expedition from the ovary through the Fallopian tubes to the uterus, an unseen equivalent of going down the Mississippi on a raft or over Niagara Falls in a barrel. Ordinarily too, the ovum travels singly, like Lewis *or* Clark, in the kind of existential loneliness which Norman Mailer usually admires. One might say that the activity of ova involves a daring and independence absent, in fact, from the activity of spermatozoa, which move in jostling masses,

* Thelma McCormick (in "Styles in Educated Females," *The Nation*, January 23, 1967, p. 118) has commented on this parallel of Bettelheim's between intellectual and sexual roles.

13

swarming out on signal like a crowd of commuters from the 5:15. The physiological contrast of apathy and enthusiasm might reasonably shift to one of individualism and conformity.

Within the same analogical convention, we assume it is necessary to escape from feminine influence if intellectual activity is to be free, inventive and original. This in turn is related to the conception of birth as a welcome release from the uterus into life—or, for the less sanguine, from the uterus into death:

> I am being given, if I may venture the expression, birth to into death, such is my impression. The feet are clear already, of the great cunt of existence. Favorable presentation I trust. My head will be the last to die.*

In either case, the child gets "clear," he is freed. Naturally then, the essence of perversity is to refuse birth. I remember a short story in which a sluggard, at full term, will not come out of the uterus, and just sits there for years and years. Eventually the mother is reconciled to this inconvenience and, as the child learns to talk, the two chat together quite amicably. They sleep at the same time, too—a social contract which of course cannot be made with the normal foetus. I dwell on this bizarre conception of the uterus as an inorganic shelter—a camping type like Robert Frost thinks of the woman as a silken *tent*—because it explains the common conception of the female mind as another domestic

* Samuel Beckett, *Malone Dies*, in *Molloy*, *Malone Dies* and *The Unnamable* (New York, Grove Press, 1959), p. 391.

14

container of some sort, a recipe file or Thermos jug or umbrella stand (cf. Jung's "ovens and cooking vessels"), always as an empty object in which others put things. (It is irrelevant that all minds are empty objects at birth, and that many minds of both sexes retain this condition in maturity.) Again of course, the physiological truth is either unknown or unnerving—that is, if one is to anthropomorphize responsibly, the uterus is a ruthless organ. Birth is not the loss but the dismissal of the foetus: the house brutally evicts the tenant. Thus, the most melodramatic action of the uterus, like that of the penis, is one of ejaculation. But it is almost an index of talent to see birth without preconception, as in Dylan Thomas's line, spoken by the mother to the newborn child, "O my lost love bounced from a good home."

It is perhaps the first and more attractive concept of the uterus as a kitchen, a place in which to be fed, that prompts another representative analogy between the female body and mental activity. In the speculations upon the female mind which I have mentioned, the omission of any reference to *creativity* is noticeable. Nothing, as far as I know, is ever created in a tent or a temple. The route of association is almost exclusively that of confinement, someone or something is locked in the kitchen. But a parallel habit of association, between childbirth and the male mind, is quite different. For some, as for Henry James, reality assumes the female role, the artist is then its grim lover: "The terrible law of the artist, the law of fructification, of fertilization." But

15

more often, the uterus alters its sex and character, and becomes a creative force of an autogenetic variety. The male uterus-mind, engaged in the production of some work, usually a work of art, seldom seems to have required the impetus of fertilization. When it does, topsy-turvily, the fertilization is conducted by the female. D. H. Lawrence provides an instance: when Lady Ottoline Morrell "moved men's imagination," she did "perhaps the most a woman can do." The woman's function is to *inspire* the man, whereupon he proceeds to develop and eventually to produce his completed work.

In writing, this analogy is responsible for that vast body of comparisons, on which a moratorium will shortly be set by the government,* of the imagination to the womb (Joyce: "O! In the virgin womb of the imagination the word was made flesh"), of slow and arduous composition to pregnancy, and of publication to the ordeal and triumph of delivery (Lovelace to Eldred Revett: "That to thine own self hast the midwife played"). At the same time, all unfinished works are abortions:

> *Amen.*
> *I have killed a poem. Killed it, unborn.*
> *To hell with it!* †

Even a fiasco is a baby, in the sense of "That's his baby." And childbirth giving inevitably onto parenthood, William

---

* The Supreme Court has already ruled on this point: the constitutional right of domestic tranquillity is *not* insured by these comparisons.
† Andrei Vozneshensky, "Lament for Two Unborn Poems."

Manchester was obliged to describe his troubles with *The Death of a President* in these terms:

> I had to fight for it. . . . It was like my child. Wouldn't a parent dash into a burning house to save his child from the flames? That was the way it was.*

A particularly dreary instance of the mode. Balzac is better:

> To pass from conception to execution, to produce, to bring the idea to birth, to raise the child laboriously from infancy, to put it nightly to sleep surfeited, to kiss it in the mornings with the hungry heart of a mother, to clean it, to clothe it fifty times over in new garments which it tears and casts away, and yet not revolt against the trials of this agitated life—this unwearying maternal love, this habit of creation—this is execution and its toils.†

But in all instances, there appears the intellectual equivalent of the *couvade*, the imagined motherhood of the male. Typically, women and children are replaced by idiots in Bernard Malamud's title "Idiots First"—so that a man with an idiot may assume the obsessive concern of the mother for the welfare of the child. And *The Fixer* is a more subtle *couvade*, a novel in which the heroism is that of a spiritual pregnancy. Jakov Bok, we are steadily told, does not seek out or demand his ordeal, he receives it. Once it is within

* *New York Times*, January 23, 1967, p. 1.
† In another context, both this and the quotation from James are discussed by Tillie Olsen in her article "SILENCES: When Writers Don't Write," *Harper's*, October 1965, p. 156.

17

him, or he within it, the external world fades away; there is nothing but the captured enclosed waiting for an unlikely, an unbearably postponed delivery. The virtues of Bok are those of the pregnant woman: endurance, patience, the gradual growth and focussing of purpose. The end of the book is the incipient delivery: Bok is on his way to some kind of birth.

We assume that femininity must disparage, but I do not mean to disparage the considerable empathy with which readers have followed Bok's ordeal. I only indicate its passive, and probably for that reason modern, ethic. But the feminine character of Bok's experience helps to explain as well the uneasy position of women in the novel. Within the large metaphor of the *couvade*, specific women characters are obliged to appear as intruders or enemies or traitors. The visible manifestations of femininity are then offensive, and so Bok experiences an acute revulsion from the sight of the woman Zina's menstrual blood. This revulsion is attributed to religious taboo, to the Talmudic injunction against sexual intercourse during menstruation. But Bok's physical horror is more intense than the injunction, which is basically humane in its origin, could explain. In fact, the mere recollection of the rule, for an audience which Malamud knows to have forgotten or never heard the rule, is revelatory. Historical verisimilitude, yes, but psychological bias too.

The Fixer is an eccentric struggle with femininity, which the hero personally assumes in its heroic aspects while he continues to retreat from its physical aspects. Blood is central to this struggle (images of blood are too purposeful, obtrusively planted, throughout the story), and particularly menstrual blood. Bok is revolted by the woman's menstruation, and by the prison guards' examination of himself for evidence of the same phenomenon. He is humiliated by this examination as a part of the Russian anti-Semitic myth; he is consciously masculine in his hatred of the bigot's conception of the Jew's effeminacy. The hatred of that accusation of womanness in the man seems natural; what distorts it is the equivalent distaste for womanness in the woman. And what accounts for that? A revulsion from all that is associated with the unjust accusation, but also a subliminal sense in which Bok has quietly and yet splendidly expropriated all that is conventionally admirable in femininity. Not one or the other, since it is impossible to read the scene with the woman Zina without recognizing an impropriety more profound than her own. This is an animosity toward physical nature which might be proper in a Swiftian context, but which disturbs a context presumably committed to a humble affirmation of human life. In Malamud's other novels as well (those which do not involve the analysis of Russian anti-Semitism), one encounters that same emotional coveting of the *ideals* of femininity in the hero, the same rejection of actual femininity. The scene with Zina in *The Fixer* recalls the parallel scene in *A New Life*, in which again the hero is revolted by the woman's body (in this case, she has a breast tumor) and again refuses sexual intercourse. There is perhaps no more representative sexual sequence in Malamud than the faint initial desire effortlessly supplanted by the objections of a superior taste or superior principle.* The hero enjoys a singular autonomy, an exceptional relief from sexual dependence, since emotionally he is himself the best of both sexes.

I suppose that Malamud's closed sexual sphere is also an indirect statement, again extraordinary, of another ordinary sexual analogy, the analogy based upon the psychoanalytic concept of bisexuality. The peculiarity of this analogy lies in its reversal of direction: as the others move from physical fact or half-fact to emotional or intellectual opinion, the bisexual analogy moves from psychoanalytic theory back to a concrete (and rather engaging) image of little bodies inside big bodies, like those wooden dolls with wooden dolls inside them. The Freudian concept has come to mean (so literally!) that somewhere inside men, on the appendix or the spleen, tiny women are crouching all the time, quiet and hidden but *there*. Freud himself balanced at the same tilt of interpretation in his lecture on Femininity. In attempting to persuade his audience, which is fixed forever now as a group of reluctant men, that bisexuality is certain in all human beings, he too resorted to a physical analogy. The audience must think of the human body: though it seems to its inhabitant solid and firm, the body is known to contain a great deal of water. What is transparent in the passage is that solidity is male, liquidity female. In effect, Freud agreed

---

* Malamud shares this fantasy of rejection with various of his contemporaries. The old animal drama of male pursuit does not hold. Instead now, women tend to offer and men to refuse—or to be incapable of accepting or to regret having accepted.

with his listeners that it is painful to acknowledge the formless feminine element in the male psyche; he merely urged acceptance of the disagreeable fact.

Most comments upon bisexuality have not since disturbed Freud's view of the matter.* So far as women are perceived also to be bisexual, they are disliked. The evidence in women of what is considered any masculine propensity is felt to be unpleasant, prompted by envy (Freud again) or excessive ambition. On one level of diction such women are called *pushy* or *driving*, on another *phallic*. And of course this last term is, in these contexts, always reproachful: men may congratulate themselves upon the productivity of their own mental wombs, but they are displeased to come upon women with mental penises.

Ordinarily, however, the folk concern with bisexuality involves men: women are women but men are men with a female component. Again there is often a small vanity about this doubleness, a kind of embarrassed pleasure in the admission. Geoffrey Gorer speaks of the woman or mother "encapsulated" in the man's nature,† and Federico Fellini's

---

* It is interesting that Jung appears to arrive at the principle of feminine bisexuality only as a logical consequence of having arrived at the principle of male bisexuality: "Since the anima is an archetype that is manifest in men, *it is reasonable to suppose that an equivalent* archetype must be present in women; for just as the man is compensated by a feminine element, so woman is compensated by a masculine one. . . ." [My italics.] *The Collected Works of C. G. Jung*, translated by R. F. C. Hull (New York, Pantheon Books, 1959), Vol. IX, part 2, p. 13.

† Geoffrey Gorer, *The American People* (New York, W. W. Norton Co., 1948), p. 56.

21

women are "the darkest part of ourselves, the undeveloped part, the true mystery within." Something digestive, even bilious, about this remark suggests an equation between women and food, rather like Tolstoy's comparison of taking two wives to eating two dinners.* But for the moment, I want only to consider the emphasis upon the primitive, the "undeveloped," as the female component. One might take as an exemplary expression of this theme a remark made by Arthur Gold in the course of his reviewing Violette Leduc's *La Bâtarde*:

> But the nervous girl who has been reappearing in my classes
> is a part of myself (as there is in every fat man a thin man try-
> ing to get out, so there is a nervous freshman girl, biting her
> fingernails, eating too much candy, and living too intensely, in

---

* The obverse association is also common: alienations from women tend toward disturbances of appetite. When, in *The Awakening* by Kate Chopin, the wife makes clear her indifference to former duties (such as receiving the wives of business associates), the husband gets up from the table, complaining that the fish is scorched, and leaves to eat dinner at his club.

Similarly, in Norman Mailer's discussions of food, its *cooking* (which is conventionally assigned to women) is ignored. The food seems to arrive, as food does in a hospital, out of some impersonal void; and Mailer's only concern with it is like the patient's only concern: *Can J get it down? And how will J feel when it's there?* In fact, Mailer's vision of intestinal conflict (between the ego and its intake) exactly parallels his vision of sexual conflict (between the ego and its partner). Just as Rojack, in *An American Dream*, thinks "Women must murder us unless we possess them altogether," so the enzymes, in *Cannibals and Christians*, seem to say, "Frogs' legs must murder us unless we digest them altogether."

each of us, no matter how Ciceronian our prose) and the value of Violette Leduc's autobiography is that it *does* this girl, once and for all.*

Rueful, but good-tempered. A wry, and yet manly, facing of the facts: there *is* a mini-girl eating jelly beans inside every one of us Ciceros.

Finally, at the same time that the male mind can choose to function periodically like a uterus, it is assumed to function primarily like a penis. Its fundamental character is seen to be aggression, and this quality is held essential to the highest or best working of the intellect. Jobs must be tackled, objections overruled, problems attacked, difficulties overcome, and offensives must always be seized. Even Lee Oswald, as his mother has recalled, was taught by one of her husbands to make his point of view clear through physical action. The conviction is generally expressed that it is more admirable to initiate or to coerce than to respond, to display rather than to conceal, to force rather than to persuade, to be serious rather than comic. So Anthony Burgess has stated his virile objections to the novels of Jane Austen:

> But now having formed my sensibility a different way, I recognize that I can gain no pleasure from serious reading (I would evidently have to take Jane Austen seriously) that lacks a strong male thrust, an almost pedantic allusiveness, and a brutal intellectual content.†

* Arthur Gold, "A woman is to crave," *Book Week*, November 7, 1965, p. 5.
† Anthony Burgess, "The Book Is Not for Reading," *New York Times Book Review*, December 4, 1966, pp. 1 and 74.

It would seem indecent to intrude on Burgess's reading experiences if he himself were not eager to describe them, thrust by thrust, in the *New York Times*. While Norman Mailer shares this sexual conception of the novel and its emphasis upon the masculine values of the genre, he shifts, in his "Great Bitch," the novel's gender:

> We've all had a piece of her, Nelson Algren, Jack Kerouac, myself . . . [a list of 34 other warty-lad novelists follows here] . . . and how many others I've missed, and all the women, all the lady writers, bless them. But one cannot speak of a woman having a piece of the Bitch.*

But of course Mailer represents only one point of view. If arrangements of words are to be judged sexually, then all sexual preferences can contribute to our critical enlightenment. Allen Ginsberg praises a haiku of Issa:

> *O ant*
> *crawl up Mount Fujiyama,*
> *but slowly, slowly.*

Now you have the small ant and you have Mount Fujiyama and you have the slowly, slowly, and what happens is that you feel almost like . . . a cock in your mouth! You feel this enormous space-universe, it's almost a tactile thing.†

It is understandable that relief from such conceptions of the artistic or intellectual act should depend upon a concept

* Norman Mailer, *Cannibals and Christians*, p. 105.
† Allen Ginsberg, *Paris Review* Interview, Spring 1966, p. 29.

of delicacy, upon a dichotomy between thought and grace. Having conceived of the mind as elemental, one must at once depreciate and delight in the supposed mindlessness of women. So Anthony Burgess, unable to consider Jane Austen, is also unable to enjoy one of her studious counterparts, Brigid Brophy. Here, suddenly, there is *too much* learning, too much rugged content: Miss Brophy's logic is not "lovable." * The objection echoes, a hundred years later, Freud's objection to John Stuart Mill's proposals for the education of women, which had come to the attention of his fiancée, Martha Bernays. For Freud too, the mind was an instrument of aggression, and education the learning of systems of attack—which given to women would, he feared, destroy the man's ideal of their *delicacy*.

The vision of intellectual effort was so thoroughly potent that it was in Freud's view naturally succeeded by periods of depletion and depression. As a young man, he expected to regress periodically into a state of mind which required the sedation of the delicate (Martha Bernays) or, failing that, the restitution of the comic (for a time, Cervantes). Failing both, Freud seems to have undergone his recurrent "neurasthenia" fatalistically, as the inevitable consequence of intellectuality. Similarly, in Tolstoy's *War and Peace*, the particular pleasure of the woman's mind is called its "spirituality," i.e., its separation from the purposeful and productive world of masculine thought, a separation which in the

* Anthony Burgess, Review of Brigid Brophy's *Don't Never Forget*, *Manchester Guardian Weekly*, November 24, 1966, p. 11.

Countess Maria is proven by the *needlessness*, the busy well-meant senselessness of the opinions and ideas she records in her diary. The same virtue of dedicated imbecility is celebrated in Natasha as the young mother, who studies nothing but the contents of soiled diapers.

❧ II ❧

PHALLIC CRITICISM

"This Neary that does not love Miss Counihan, nor need his Needle, any more, may he soon get over Murphy and find himself free, following his drift, to itch for an ape, or a woman writer."

—Samuel Beckett, *Murphy*

◆§ Through practice, begun when they begin to read, women learn to read about women calmly. Perhaps there have been some, but I have not heard of women who killed themselves simply and entirely because they were women.* They are evidently sustained by the conviction that I can never be They, by the fact that the self always, at least to itself, eludes identification with others. And, in turn, this radical separateness is fortified in some of us by phlegm, in others by vanity or most of all by ignorance (the uneducated are humiliated by class rather than by sex)—by all the usual defenses against self-loathing. Moreover, both men and women are now particularly accustomed, not so much to the resolution of issues, as to the proliferation of irreconcilable opinions upon them. In this intellectual suspension, it is possible for women, most of the time, to be more interested in what *is* said about them than in what presumably and finally *should* be said about them. In fact, none of them knows what should be said.

Their detachment is perhaps especially useful in reading

* Men, however, have been known to kill themselves for this reason. Otto Weininger, the German author of *Sex and Character*, killed himself because of the femininity which he ascribed to the Jews, of whom he was one.

literary criticism. Here, the opinions of men about men and of women about women are at least possibly esthetic, but elsewhere they are, almost inescapably, sexual as well. Like eruptions of physical desire, this intellectual distraction is no less frequent for being gratuitous as well. With a kind of inverted fidelity, the discussion of women's books by men will arrive punctually at the point of preoccupation, which is the fact of femininity. Books by women are treated as though they themselves were women, and criticism embarks, at its happiest, upon an intellectual measuring of busts and hips. Of course, this preoccupation has its engaging and compensatory sides.* Like such minor physical disorders as shingles and mumps, it often seems (whether or not it *feels* to the critic) comical as well as distressing. Then too, whatever intellectual risks this criticism runs, one of them is not abstraction. Any sexual reference, even in the most dryasdust context, shares the power which any reference to food has, of provoking fresh and immediate interest. As lunch can be mentioned every day without boring those

* It has an unnerving side as well, though this appears less often in criticism, I think, than in fiction or poetry. For example, James Dickey's poem "Falling" expresses an extraordinary concern with the underwear of a woman who has fallen out of an airplane. While this woman, a stewardess, was in the airplane, her girdle obscured, to the observation of even the most alert passenger, her mesial groove. The effect was, as the poem recalls, "monobuttocked." As the woman falls, however, she undresses and "passes her palms" over her legs, her breasts, and "deeply between her thighs." Beneath her, "widowed farmers" are soon to wake with futile (and irrelevant?) erections. She lands on her back in a field, naked, and dies. The sensation of the poem is necrophilic: it mourns a vagina rather than a person crashing to the ground.

29

who are hungry, the critic can always return to heterosexual (and, increasingly, to homosexual) relations and opinions with certainty of being read.

Admittedly, everyone is amused by the skillful wrapping of a book, like a negligee, about an author. Stanley Kauffmann opened a review of Françoise Sagan's *La Chamade* with this simile:

> Poor old Françoise Sagan. Just one more old-fashioned old-timer, bypassed in the rush for the latest literary vogue and for youth. Superficially, her career in America resembles the lifespan of those medieval beauties who flowered at 14, were deflowered at 15, were old at 30 and crones at 40.*

A superior instance of the mode—the play, for example, between *flowered* and *deflowered* is neat. And quite probably, of course, women might enjoy discussing men's books in similar terms. Some such emulative project would be diverting for a book season or two, if it were possible to persuade conventional journals to print its equivalent remarks. From a review of a new novel by the popular French novelist, François Sagan:

> Poor old François Sagan. . . . Superficially, his career in America resembles the life-span of those medieval troubadours who masturbated at 14, copulated at 15, were impotent at 30 and prostate cases at 40.

Somehow or other, No. It is not that male sexual histories, in themselves, are not potentially funny—even though they

* Stanley Kauffmann, "Toujours Tristesse," *New Republic*, October 29, 1966, p. 2.

seem to be thought perceptibly less so than female sexual histories. It is rather that the literal fact of masculinity, unlike femininity, does not impose an erogenic form upon all aspects of the person's career.

I do not mean to suggest, however, that this imposition necessarily results in injustice. (Stanley Kauffmann went on to be more than just, *merciful* to Françoise Sagan.) In fact, it sometimes issues in fulsome praise. Excess occurs when the critic, like Dr. Johnson congratulating the dog who walked like a man, is impressed that the woman has—not so much written well, as written at all. But unfortunately, benign as this upright-pooch predisposition can be in the estimate of indifferent work, it can also infect the praise of work which deserves (what has to be called) asexual approval. In this case, enthusiasm issues in an explanation of the ways in which the work is free of what the critic ordinarily dislikes in the work of a woman. He had despaired of ever seeing a birdhouse built by a woman; now *here* is a birdhouse built by a woman. Pleasure may mount even to an admission of male envy of the work examined: an exceptionally sturdy birdhouse at that! In *Commentary*, Warren Coffey has expressed his belief that "a man would give his right arm to have written Flannery O'Connor's 'Good Country People.' "* And here, not only the sentiment but the confidence with which the cliché is wielded, is distinctly phallic. It is as though, merely by thinking about Flannery O'Connor or Mrs. Gaskell or Harriet Beecher Stowe, the critic experienced acute sensations of his own liberty. The

* Warren Coffey, *Commentary*, November 1965, p. 98.

more he considers a feeble, cautious and timid existence, the more devil-may-care he seems to himself. This exhilaration then issues, rather tamely, in a daring to be commonplace.

And curiously, it often issues in expressions of contempt for delicate men as well. In this piece, for example, Flannery O'Connor is praised not only as a woman writer who writes as well as a man might wish to write, but also as a woman writer who succeeds in being less feminine than some men. She is less "girlish" than Truman Capote or Tennessee Williams.* In effect, once the critic's attention is trained, like Sweeney's, upon the Female Temperament, he invariably sideswipes at effeminacy in the male as well. The basic distinction becomes nonliterary: it is less between the book under review and other books, than between the critic and other persons who seem to him, regrettably, less masculine than he is. The assumption of the piece is that no higher praise of a woman's work exists than that such a critic should like it or think that other men will like it. The same ploy can also be executed in reverse. Norman Mailer, for example, is pleased to think that Joseph Heller's *Catch-22* is a man's book to read, a book which merely "puzzles" women. Women cannot comprehend male books, men cannot tolerate female books. The working rule is simple, basic:

* Though Tennessee Williams is cited here to enhance Flannery O'Connor's virtues, he is just as easily cited to prove other women's defects. For example, Dr. Karl Stern has resorted to Williams and Edward Albee as witnesses to the modern prevalence of the Castrating Woman. (*Barat Review*, January 1967, p. 46.) Naturally, in this context, both playwrights assume a status of unqualified virility.

there must always be two literatures like two public toilets, one for Men and one for Women.

Sometimes it seems that no achievement can override this division. When Marianne Moore received the Poetry Society of America's Gold Medal for Poetry, she received as well Robert Lowell's encomium, "She is the best woman poet in English." The late Langston Hughes added, "I consider her the most famous Negro woman poet in America," and others would have enjoyed "the best blue-eyed woman poet."* Lowell has also praised Sylvia Plath's last book of poems, *Ariel*. His foreword begins:

> In these poems, written in the last months of her life and often rushed out at the rate of two or three a day, Sylvia Plath becomes herself, becomes something imaginary, newly, wildly and subtly created—hardly a person at all, or a woman, certainly not another "poetess," but one of those super-real, hypnotic, great classical heroines. The character is feminine, rather than female, though almost everything we customarily think of as feminine is turned on its head. The voice is now coolly amused, witty, now sour, now fanciful, girlish, charming, now sinking to the strident rasp of the vampire—a Dido, Phaedra, or Medea, who can laugh at herself as "cow-heavy and floral in my Victorian nightgown."

* Miss Moore's femininity leaves her vulnerable even to the imagination of John Berryman:

> *Fancy a lark with Sappho,*
> *a tumble in the bushes with Miss Moore,*
> *a spoon with Emily, while Charlotte glare.*
> *Miss Bishop's too noble-O.*

("Four Dream Songs," *Atlantic*, February 1968, p. 68.)

A little cloudburst, a short heavy rain of sexual references. The word *poetess*, whose gender killed it long ago, is exhumed—to be denied. Equivalently, a critic of W. H. Auden would be at pains, first of all, to deny that Auden is a poetaster. But *poetess* is only part of the general pelting away at the single fact that Sylvia Plath belonged to a sex (that inescapable membership) and that her sex was not male—*woman, heroines, feminine, female, girlish, fanciful, charming, Dido, Phaedra, Medea. Vampire*, too. And it would of course be this line, "Cow-heavy and floral in my Victorian nightgown," which seizes attention first and evokes the surprised pleasure of realizing that Sylvia Plath "can laugh at herself." Self-mockery, particularly sexual self-mockery, is not expected in a woman, and it is irresistible in the criticism of women to describe what was expected: the actual seems to exist only in relation to the preconceived.

Lowell's distinction between *feminine* and *female* is difficult, though less difficult than a distinction between *masculine* and *male* would be—say, in an introduction to Blake's *Songs of Innocence*. What helps us with the first is our all knowing, for some time now, that femaleness is a congenital fault, rather like eczema or Original Sin. An indicative denunciation, made in 1889: "They are no ladies. The only word good enough for them is the word of opprobrium—females." But fortunately, some women can be saved. By good manners, they are translated from females into ladies; and by talent, into feminine creatures (or even into "classical heroines"). And we are entirely accustomed to this generic mobility on their part: the individual is assumed into the sex and loses all but typical meaning within it. The emphasis is finally macabre, as though women wrote with breasts instead of pens—in which event it would be remarkable, as Lowell feels that it is, if one of them achieved ironic detachment.

When the subject of the work by a woman is also women (as it often has to be, since everyone has to eat what's in the cupboard), its critical treatment is still more aberrant. Like less specialized men, critics seem to fluctuate between attraction and surfeit. An obsessive concern with femininity shifts, at any moment, into a sense of being confined or suffocated by it. In the second condition, a distaste for books *before they are read* is not uncommon, as in Norman Mailer's unsolicited confession of not having been able to read Virginia Woolf, or in Anthony Burgess's inhibitory "impression of high-waisted dresses and genteel parsonage flirtation"* in Jane Austen's novels. More luckily, the work may be patronized by mild minds already persuaded that the human temperament combines traits of both sexes and that even masculine natures may respond, through their subterranean femininity, to the thoroughly feminine book.

A similar indulgence is fostered by any association, however tenuous, which the critic forms between the woman writer and some previous student of his own.† Now that almost everyone who writes teaches too, the incidence of this association is fairly high. Robert Lowell remembers

---

* *New York Times Book Review*, December 4, 1966, p. 1.
† For the especial amicability of this sexual relationship, see "The Student," p. 119.

that Sylvia Plath once audited a class of his at Boston University:

> She was never a student of mine, but for a couple of months seven years ago, she used to drop in on my poetry seminar at Boston University. I see her dim against the bright sky of a high window, viewless unless one cared to look down on the city outskirts' defeated yellow brick and square concrete pillbox filling stations. She was willowy, long-waisted, sharp-elbowed, nervous, giggly, gracious—a brilliant tense presence embarrassed by restraint. Her humility and willingness to accept what was admired seemed at times to give her an air of maddening docility that hid her unfashionable patience and boldness.*

It is not easy, of course, to write about a person whom one knew only slightly in the past. The strain is felt here, for example, in the gratuitous street scene from the classroom window. And in general, there is a sense of a physical recollection emended by a much later intellectual and poetic impression. The "brilliant tense presence" of the final poetry is affixed, generously enough, to the original figure of a young girl. The "maddening docility" too must have been a sexual enlargement, now reduced to an "air" of docility, since again the poems demonstrate the artistic (rather than "feminine") union of "patience and boldness." (Elsewhere they are, according to Lowell, "modest" poems too, they are uniquely "modest" *and* "bold.") But then the poet Anne Sexton's recollections, which originate in the same poetry

---

* Foreword to Sylvia Plath's *Ariel*, p. xi.

seminar, make no reference to elbows or giggles or docility. Miss Sexton seems to have seen even at that time a woman entirely congruous with her later work. After class, the two used to drink together—at the Ritz bar, some distance away from those "concrete pillbox filling stations"—and conduct workmanlike discussions of suicidal techniques:

> But suicides have a special language.
> Like carpenters they want to know which tools.
> They never ask why build.
>
> ("Wanting to Die") *

Lowell seems honestly caught between two ways of comprehending what exists outside the self. And certainly there is nothing of the stag posture about his remarks, no pretense of writing only for other men about women. All critics are of course secretly aware that no literary audience, except perhaps in Yemen, is any longer restricted to men. The man's-man tone is a deliberate archaism, coy and even flirtatious, like wearing spats. No one doubts that some silent misogyny may be dark and deep, but written misogyny is now generally a kind of chaffing, and not frightfully clever, gambit. For the critic in this style, the writer whose work is most easily related to established stereotypes of femininity is, oddly, the most welcome. What-to-say then flows effortlessly from the stereotypes themselves. The word *feminine* alone, like a grimace, expresses a displeasure which is not less certain for its being undefined. In a review of Fawn

* Anne Sexton, "The barfly ought to sing," *Tri-Quarterly*, Fall 1966, p. 90.

Brodie's biography of Sir Richard Burton, *The Devil Drives*, Josh Greenfeld remarked on the "feminine biographer's attachment to subject," and suggested that this quality (*or else* a "scholarly objectivity") prevented Mrs. Brodie's conceding Burton's homosexuality.* So her book is either too subjective or too objective: we will never know which.

But the same word can be turned upon men too. John Weightman has remarked that Genet's criminals cannot play male and female effectively because "a convicted criminal, however potent, has been classified as an object, and therefore feminized, by society." † An admirably simple social equation: a man in prison amounts to a woman. Similarly, *feminine* functions as an eight-letter word in the notorious Woodrow Wilson biography by Freud and William Bullitt. At one heated point, Clemenceau calls Wilson feminine, Wilson calls Clemenceau feminine, then both Freud and Bullitt call Wilson feminine again. The word means that all four men thoroughly dislike each other. It is also sufficient for Norman Mailer to say that Herbert Gold reminds him "of nothing so much as a woman writer," ‡ and for Richard Gilman to consign Philip Roth to the "ladies' magazine"

---

* *Book Week*, May 28, 1967, p. 2. Mrs. Brodie had still more trouble in the *Times Literary Supplement* (January 11, 1968, p. 32), where her nationality as well as her sex was at fault: "So immense is this gulf, so inalienably remote are the societies that produced biographer and subject, *so difficult is it, even now, for a woman to get beneath a man's skin*, that only some imaginative genius could really have succeeded in the task Mrs. Brodie so boldly undertook." [My italics.]
† *New York Review of Books*, August 24, 1967, p. 8.
‡ *Advertisements for Myself*, p. 435.

level.* In fact, chapters of *When She Was Good* were first published, and seemed to settle in snugly, at the *haut bourgeois* level of *Harper's* and the *Atlantic*. But, except perhaps in the *Daily Worker*, the consciousness of class is less insistent than that of sex: the phrase "ladies' magazine" is one of those which refuses not to be written once a month.†

But at heart most of these "the-ladies-bless-them" comments are as cheerful and offhand as they are predictable. When contempt, like anything else, has an assigned route to follow, and when it is accustomed to its course, it can proceed happily. This is evident, for example, in Norman Mailer's lively, even jocular, essay on the deplorable faults of Mary McCarthy's *The Group*. What accounts for these high spirits, except the fact that Mailer rejoices in what he spanks so loudly? The pleasure lies in Mary McCarthy's having capitulated, as it seems to Mailer, having at last written what he can securely and triumphantly call a female novel.‡ Not that Mailer's treatment of *The Group*, even in

* Richard Gilman, "Let's Lynch Lucy," *New Republic*, June 24, 1967, p. 19.

† The phrase is at least sociologically interesting: it suggests the impossibility of remarking that some bad novel is fit for the "men's magazine." For fiction, there is none. At the same level of intelligence and cultivation, women evidently prefer stories (*McCall's, Redbook, The Ladies' Home Journal*, etc.) and men prefer facts (or quasi-facts) and photographs (*Time, Life, Look, Dude, Gent*, etc.). *Playboy* is exceptional in presupposing an eclectic male audience (does it exist?) for both photographs *and* fiction.

‡ A female novel, Mailer indicates, is one which deals with the superficial details of women's lives instead of their lower depths. Such a book is at once tedious and cowardly. On the other hand, Joseph Heller's

these familiar terms, is not still remarkable—even frightening, and that is a rare treat in criticism. One does not expect a disdain for feminine concerns, which is entirely commonplace, to mount to cloacal loathing. Mary McCarthy has soiled an abstraction, a genre, the novel-yet-to-be: "Yes, Mary deposited a load on the premise, and it has to be washed all over again, this little long-lived existential premise".*

But few rise to that kind of washing-up with Mailer's alacrity. In most critics, revulsion is an under-developed area. What rouses a much more interesting hostility in many is the work which does not conform to sexual preconception. That is, if feminine concerns can be found, they are conventionally rebuked; but their absence is shocking. While all women's writing should presumably strive for a suprafeminine condition, it is profoundly distrusted for achieving it. So for all Anthony Burgess's resistance to Jane Austen, he is still less pleased by George Eliot ("The male impersonation is wholly successful") or by Ivy Compton-Burnett ("A big sexless nemesic force"). Similarly, he cannot leave alone what strikes him as the contradiction between Brigid

---

Catch-22 is a book for men (rather than a male novel) which deals with the superficial details of men's lives. It speaks, according to Mailer, to the man who "prefers to become interested in quick proportions and contradictions; in the practical surface of things." Both novels, then, are tedious but the first is a disgrace while the second has "a vast appeal." Obviously, it all depends on which practical surface of things the commentator himself is glued to.

* *Cannibals and Christians*, p. 138.

Brophy's appearance and her writing.* His review of her book of essays, *Don't Never Forget*, opens in this sprightly manner:

> An American professor friend of mine, formerly an admirer of Miss Brophy's work, could no longer think of her as an author once he'd seen her in the flesh. "That girl was made for love," he would growl. Various writers who have smarted from her critical attentions might find it hard to agree.†

It is as though Elizabeth Hardwick, asked to review William Manchester's *Death of a President*, was obliged to refuse, growling, "That man was made for love." The same notion of an irreconcilable difference between the nature of woman and the mind of man prompts the hermaphroditic fallacy according to which one half the person, separating from the

* Burgess has also furnished this country, in a "Letter from London" (*Hudson Review*, Spring 1967), the following couplet:
> People who read Brigid Brophy
> Should contend for the Krafft-Ebing Trophy.

In fact, he seems unfailingly exhilarated by Miss Brophy's faults, thrilled by them as Norman Mailer is by Mary McCarthy's. Burgess's most recent agitation was a review of *Fifty Works of English Literature We Could Do Without* (by Miss Brophy, Michael Levey and Charles Osborne): "The authors are now rubbing themselves in an ecstacy of the kind granted only to Exclusive Brethren." (*Encounter*, August 1967, p. 71.)

† *Manchester Guardian Weekly*, November 24, 1966, p. 11. There is, incidentally, An American Professor who exists only in the minds of English journalists. The *Times Literary Supplement* would be halved without him.

41

other half, produces a book by binary fission. So Mary McCarthy has been complimented, though not by Norman Mailer, on her "masculine mind" while, through the ages, poor Virgil has never been complimented on his "effeminacy." (Western criticism begins with this same tedious distinction—between manly Homer and womanish Virgil.) At the same time, while sentiment is a disadvantage, the alternative of feminine coolness is found still more disagreeable. Mary McCarthy used to be too *formidable*, Jean Stafford has sometimes been *clinical*, and others (going down, down) are *perverse, petulant, catty, waspish*.

The point is that comment upon Violette Leduc, who is not directly assertive, will be slurring; but the slur hardens into resentment of those writers who seem to endorse the same standards of restraint and reason which the critic presumably endorses. If for nothing else, for her tolerance of Sade, Simone de Beauvoir must be referred to (scathingly!) as "the lady," and then even her qualifications of tolerance must be described as a reluctance "to give herself unreservedly" to Sade.* Similarly, it is possible that much of the voluble male distaste for Jane Austen is based, not upon her military limitations (her infamous failure to discuss the Napoleonic Wars), but upon her antipathetic detachment. So a determined counteremphasis was first placed by her relatives, and has been continued since by most of her critics, upon her allegiance to domestic ideals—when, in fact, she is read only for her mockery of them.

What seems to be wanted, insisted upon, is the critic's

* Leslie Schaeffer, *New Republic*, August 19, 1967, p. 28.

conception of women expressed in his conception of feminine terms—that is, a confirmation of the one sex's opinions by the imagination of the other, a difficult request which can seldom be gratified. It is perhaps this request which explains Louis Auchincloss's erratic view of Mary McCarthy in his *Pioneers and Caretakers*. Suddenly she is sister to Ellen Glasgow and Sarah Orne Jewett, as one of our feminine "caretakers of the culture," a guise in which few other readers can easily recognize her. But if one's thesis is sexual, the attachment of women to the past and the incapacity of women for "the clean sweep," then Mary McCarthy only seems to hate a few present things and actually loves many past things. One might as well argue that it was Swift's finding babies so sweet that made him think of eating them for dinner.

The vague and ominous critical implications of femininity, with which we generally make do now, were more precisely defined by Walter Pater:

Manliness in art, what can it be, as distinct from that which in opposition to it must be called the feminine quality there,—what but a full consciousness of what one does, of art itself in the work of art, tenacity of intuition and of consequent purpose, the spirit of construction as opposed to what is literally incoherent or ready to fall to pieces, and, in opposition to what is hysteric or works at random, the maintenance of a standard. Of such art $\dot{\eta}\theta os$ rather than $\pi\dot{a}\theta os$ will be the predominant mood. To use Plato's own expression, there will be here no παραλειπόμενα, no "negligences," no feminine forgetfulness of one's self, nothing in the work of art unconformed to the leading intention of the artist, who will but increase his power by reserve. An artist of this kind will be apt, of course, to express more than he seems actually to say. He economizes. He will not spoil good things by exaggeration. The rough, promiscuous wealth of nature he reduces to grace and order: reduces, it may be, lax verse to staid and temperate prose. With him, the rhythm, the music, the notes, will be felt to follow, or rather literally accompany as ministers, the sense,— ἀκολονθεῖν τόν λόγον.*

The intellectual consequences of unmanliness are prodigal. The feminine is the not fully conscious, not fully assembled, the intemperate, incoherent, hysterical, extravagant and capricious. In the rush of his contrasts, Pater comes to the verge of dismissing poetry: "verse" is a slut, and "staid, temperate prose" is a don. A limited view of the two forms, but understandable in the light of Pater's own twin employments as lecturer on the Renaissance and prose stylist. "The rough, promiscuous wealth of nature" anticipates (unlikely as any association between the two may seem) such a later fancy as Leslie Fiedler's image of the sculpture as male, and the tree out of which the sculpture is carved, as female. Here

---

* Walter Pater, "Plato's Esthetics," *Plato and Platonism* (New York, 1899), pp. 253–54. The only term associated with women which Pater seems to have enjoyed was *pregnancy*, and that only in references to men instead: "Goethe, then in all the pregnancy of his wonderful youth. . . ." (*The Renaissance*, Cleveland and New York, The World Publishing Co., 1961, p. 193.)

too, male art imposes form upon female nature. The homosexual contrast is between two possible partners: *nature*, the coarse, indiscriminate and blowsy woman, and *art*, the ordered, graceful and exquisite boy.

Pater foreshadows our present situation, however, in that his concern for "manliness" in art expends itself as much upon the contraindications to masculinity as upon its intrinsic properties. We are now wholly familiar with this emphasis upon the difficulties, rather than the capacities, of the male artist. The same emphasis has, in fact, mounted now to a sense of armies fighting openly against his accomplishment. Danger is unanimously confirmed, only its nature or origin is less agreed upon. Philip Roth has suggested the increasing difficulty of fiction's competing with actuality. What political novelist, he asks, could *imagine* Eisenhower, who yet seems an effect casually thrown off by society? Reality, then, is inimical to the writer, having itself grown incomparably fantastic. On the other hand, Saul Bellow argues that the writer is impeded by literary intellectuals whose respect for past achievements depresses present efforts. And Norman Mailer finds that it is ubiquitous corruption which prevents art. In architecture, for example:

> There is so much corruption in the building codes, over-inflation in the value of land, featherbedding built into union rules, so much graft, so much waste, so much public relations, and so much emptiness that no one tries to do more with the roof than leave it flat.*

* *Cannibals and Christians*, p. 234.

Mailer is forever Gothic and aspirant, possessed by a vision of renewal and of total accomplishment. But meanwhile hostile forces remain in the ascendancy, suppressing and flattening talent. The threat of these forces steadily diverts the writer—not from writing, but from writing what he would write if he did not feel threatened. In self-defense, he does quasi-military exercises for writing in the future, a kind of shadow-typing until the date is set for a real match. For the time being, communiqués are issued, protesting the present and improper circumstances of art and thereby adding to them—rather as people bang on their ceilings to make the upstairs people stop banging on their floors.

I do not mean to underestimate this conviction on the part of many writers that they live among strangers and aliens. On the contrary, I am alienated in turn by the habitual identification of this complex and all-encompassing enmity with the relatively narrow circumstance of sexuality. It is through this identification that phallic criticism regularly and rapidly shifts from writing by women, which can be dismissed as innocuous, to their vicious influence upon writing by men. It is clear that sexual conflict has become the specific focus, literal as well as metaphoric, of a general and amorphous sense of intellectual conflict. A simple instance is this last novel of Philip Roth's, *When She Was Good*, in which a pimple of a young woman is created only to be squeezed, interminably, to death—a small self-gratification which none of us would deny each other, but still prefer not to witness. And yet this tiny tumor, this Emma Bovary in galoshes, is supposed to define the Morality of the Middle West. Nothing much must stand for everything.

But the metaphoric focus is ordinarily more interesting. The capacity to write, even as it is held more and more precariously, is made synonymous with sexual capacity, whereupon the woman becomes the enemy of both. She appears as the risk that the writer has to take, or the appetite, at once sluggish and gargantuan, which must be roused and then satisfied in order to prove that the writer is capable of giving satisfaction of any kind. So she is all that offers stubborn and brute resistance to achievement even as she is its only route. Her range is limitless, all internal obstacle as well as external impediment, all that within the writer himself may prevent his accomplishing his aim— weakness, dullness, caution, fear, dishonesty, triviality.

At the crudest level of this metaphoric struggle, the writer finds his professional and sexual activities incompatible, on the grounds of the distribution of resources. This anxiety seems distinctly modern. The association of the two faculties, intellectual and sexual, is ancient, but the expressed inability to reconcile them is recent. Blake, for example, celebrated "the lineaments of gratified desire," and seemed to sense no contradiction between them and artistic gratification. In fact, he considered sexual intercourse, rather like having breakfast or a walk in the garden, an essential prelude to composition. Hemingway, instead, found a young writer to warn against making love during periods of composition: the best ideas would be lost in bed. An intense frugality has

47

set in, a determination not to squander vital spirits. Goods produced or released by the self, like semen and words, become oddly equivalent and interdependent. The Samson law: the consumption or removal of one product, particularly by a woman, must inevitably diminish another. Naturally then, the minds which so balance the books of themselves frequently remark upon the materiality of women. The impression is deflected from their own sense of possessing a warehouse of scarce, conglomerate materials, all subtracting strength from each other, and all consequently in need of vigilant supervision. A loss of all one's buttons will inevitably mean a strain on one's supply of safety pins. A fear of insufficiency develops, a terror of running out. All sexual difficulties have therefore shifted in fiction from women to men, from feminine barrenness to masculine impotence or sterility or utter indifference. The women are uniformly and insatiably greedy (again, of course, in fiction) for conception. The men cannot afford to give them, indiscriminately, all the children they demand. The expenditure could only mean their going, as writers, into debtors' prison.

And yet there is an opposite dilemma: the testing of talent is confounded with the testing of sexual resources. Both must engage themselves, even though each engagement risks depletion or failure. In this metaphoric distortion, the actual energy and excess of nature is forgotten or does not convince. The rich, against all reason, describe their poverty, and every spermatozoon stands for an item of talent, infinitesimal and yet precious. It is all like (a literary) India, where men are commonly convinced of the debilitating consequences of intercourse even as the population increases by a million a month. In such a context, Milton's old cause for concern,

> *And that one talent which is death to hide*
> *Lodged with me useless,*

seems cavalier—at least the talent is eager and impatient. Instead now, the cause of death seems to be the extravagant and unguarded employment of talent. It should be housed and protected and kept ready for a crucial moment in the indefinite future. And this future engagement is envisaged as a quarrel which the fighter-lover-writer will probably lose, or (at best) a prize of which he will probably be cheated. The possibility of failure, either of one's own nerve or of the other's loyalty, is always present. The best preparation is to stockpile animosity. In this connection, Norman Mailer has described one of the prize fighter Harry Greb's "training methods":

> That is, before he had a fight he would go to a brothel, and he would have two prostitutes, not one, taking the two of them into the same bed. And this apparently left him feeling like a wild animal. Don't ask me why. Perhaps he picked the two meanest whores in the joint and so absorbed into his system all the small, nasty, concentrated evils which had accumulated from carloads of men. Greb was known as the dirtiest fighter of his time.*

The thin chance held by the fighting talent is intertwined with sexual chance, and the possibilities of subversion or

* *Cannibals and Christians*, p. 217.

treachery are contained, like mutated ova, in the female. The commonplace sexual fiction must now regularly describe a man—preferably gifted, but a fool will do in a pinch—who cannot get his work done because he is involved with a deficient woman. His abilities are either wasted on her stupidity or poisoned by her malice. No one, again, distrusted women more than Milton, and yet it was possible for him to retain a conception of at least a sombre accord, founded upon an unremitting discipline:

> *Therefore God's universal law*
> *Gave to the man despotic power*
> *Over his female in due awe,*
> *Nor from that right to part an hour*
> *Smile she or lour:*
> *So shall he least confusion draw*
> *On his whole life, not swayed*
> *By female usurpation, nor dismayed.*
> (*Samson Agonistes*, ll.1053–60)

Occasionally, Mailer attempts the terms of this past co-existence: "she had fled the domination which was liberty for her" ("The Time of Her Time"), but this is only in bed and besides the mood has collapsed. Allowed domination, or at least imaginative domination, Milton also furnished confident images of fructification. The abyss upon which the Holy Ghost broods (rather like a *hen*) is vast and yet yielding to impregnation. The abyss for Mailer is an enticing image of terror, an irresistible descent into horror. At best, it is like a point on Bunyan's map, a Pit of Responsibility. The writer descends to face truths which will diminish previous self-estimations.

Women are waiting in this pit, like large, pallid insects under stones, and whatever grace—or rather *significance*, there must always be some moral significance—the sexual encounter retains is at once masculine and dour: it is a test of courage, a persistence in the face of disgust. Conception is difficult: either the spermatozoa are wasted (thrown away! squandered! from fortune to farm) on contraceptives or they must be assisted by fury: "Satan, if it takes your pitchfork up my gut, let me blast a child into this bitch."* And yet these encounters are more intellectual than physical statements, since the effect upon women is premonitory of the effect upon words, of failure (always the more likely) or success in writing: "Every child is a poem someone conceived in short space."† (Conceived? Then a *poetess* is meant?) So the hero of Mailer's story, "The Time of Her Time," Sergius O'Shaughnessy, attaches symbolic meaning to his (hardly unparalleled) effort to bring his partner to orgasm. Achieving that, ". . . it was more likely that I would win the next time I gambled my stake on something more appropriate for my ambition."

The concept of femininity is static and resistant, that of masculinity at once dynamic and striving:

> Masculinity is not something given to you, something you're born with, but something you gain. And you gain it by winning

* *An American Dream*, p. 240.
† *Cannibals and Christians*, p. 202.

small battles with honor. Because there is very little honor left in American life, there is a certain built-in tendency to destroy masculinity.*

That is, it is difficult not only to pass a test but to find a test to pass. Everything conspires to make occasions of courage, in the formal and stylized sense of such occasions in the past, hard to come by. Hemingway was reduced to fighting fish, and the only land test in constant supply is fighting females. So armed intercourse must subsume all other single tournaments. In *An American Dream*, the mythomaniac Rojack combats social evil with his honorable penis, cousin to Sergius O'Shaughnessy's chivalric "avenger." And like O'Shaughnessy, Rojack scores by sodomy, his only way with a German housemaid of rebuking the immense social horror of Nazism.

But the avenger-writer, even as he engages with the enemy, risks deception. If the whore-novel (with her "feminine taste for the mortal wound") is not quite deadly, she is always at least devious:

> Every novelist who has slept with the Bitch (only poets and writers of short stories have a *Muse*) comes away bragging afterward like a G.I. tumbling out of a whorehouse spree— "Man, I made her moan," goes the cry of the young writer. But the Bitch laughs afterward in her empty bed. "He was so sweet in the beginning," she declares, "but by the end he just went, 'Peep, peep, peep.'" †

* *Cannibals and Christians*, p. 201.
† *Cannibals and Christians*, p. 107. From this it follows, as the belch

The sympathetic role is shuffled: the writer is the Orpheus now, too vulnerable or too impressionable not to be victimized by the cruelties of inspiration. Or deluded into vanity by false success. And worse, in having to deal with dishonesty, writers may grow dishonest too. The Bitch is full of "swilling crafts" by which they can be contaminated. The vision, then, must be of an achievement beyond craft, something wildly and spontaneously pure, beyond practice or calculation or skill. If a writer is always in training, it is nevertheless in order to accomplish something in the end which is quite alien to training. It is as though one prepared regularly, through sexual promiscuity, for the future assumption of an absolute virginity.

At the lowest level of writing as sexual act, in pornography, the exercise is frankly masturbatory. But actually, in any persistent association of the two experiences, even a metaphoric association, the impression of onanism (which is perhaps appropriate to writing) is inescapable. Mailer has almost forgiven J. D. Salinger's *Raise High the Roof Beam, Carpenters*, in these terms:

> Now, all of us have written as badly. There are nights when one comes home after a cancerously dull party, full of liquor but not drunk, leaden with boredom, somewhere out of Fitzgerald's long dark night. Writing at such a time is like making love at such a time. It is hopeless, it desecrates one's future, but one does it anyway because at least it is an act.*

---

the gas, that "a good novelist can do without everything but the remnant of his balls." (*Advertisements for Myself*, p. 435.)
* *Cannibals and Christians*, pp. 123–24.

Here, the "act" of making love is as solitary as the act of defecating or of writing, or, for that matter, of dying. ("Herr Hemingway, can you sum up your feelings about death?" and Herr Hemingway: "Yes—just another whore.") All that seems active outside the impacted consciousness, and therefore all that can pierce it, is time: hence, that familiar anxiety for abstractions like the genre or the "future." The only sensation attributed to concrete forms outside the self is implacability, an obscure inimical urge to resist domination. But some signature must be left upon these surroundings, some exertion made, even hopelessly. Encircled by blank forms, one fills them out, one writes over them. In that sense, composition and copulation are now considered identical twins.

⋅≈ III ≈⋅

FEMININE STEREOTYPES

Formlessness

Passivity

Instability

Confinement

Piety

Materiality

Spirituality

Irrationality

Compliancy

Two Incorrigible Figures:
  The Shrew and the Witch

⊷§ Even individual character is finally impenetrable, and the character, say, of an entire nation so obscure that to offer its definition is considered obscurantism, or worse. At the end of the Second World War, with the full exposure of the Germans' "Final Solution" of the Jews, it was still felt to be an intellectual impropriety to characterize the moral nature of Germany. Particularly then, since revulsion seems the least proper motive of characterization. But even those who despise the mode of thought cannot help but practice it. And a hope to repress sexual characterization, the most entrenched form of the general mode, would be as futile as a hope to end prostitution or even all sexual intercourse. There is perhaps nothing to which we are more accustomed, nothing which we digest more easily, than such an excursion as the following, from Mary McCarthy's short story, "The Genial Host":

Most Jewish men were more feminine than Gentile men of similar social background. You had noticed this and had supposed, vaguely, that it was the mark matriarchy had left on them, but looking at Pflaumen you saw the whole process dramatically. The matriarch had begun by being married off to a husband who was prosperous and settled and older than herself, and her sons she had created in her own image, forlorn little bridegrooms to a middle-aged bride.

In most of the men, the masculine influence had, in the end, overridden or absorbed the feminine, and you saw only vestigial traces of the mother. There might be a tendency to hypochondria, a readiness to take offense, personal vanity, love of comfort, love of being waited on and made much of; and, on the other hand, there would be unusual intuitive powers, sympathy, loyalty, tenderness, domestic graces and kindnesses unknown to the Gentile.

The stereotypes of feminine character are embedded within those of Jewish character, and subscription to the one lot seems entirely at home with subscription to the other.* Of course, Mary McCarthy certainly would not have wanted to write the passage, to play the poor woman's Otto Weininger, after the Second World War, when even kind generalizations about the Jews fell into extreme disrepute. Still, their characterization here takes on an illusory strength through its connection with the characterization of women, which in turn is fortified by all physical interest—of which curiosity, speculation and assertion are, for human beings, natural extensions.

These intellectual exercises are the conventional means of

* The one preoccupation seems quite generally to accompany the other. In Mailer's *An American Dream*, for example, references to Polish brutality, Irish treachery, German physiognomy, etc., occur almost as regularly as generic references to women. And all Leslie Fiedler's characters, men and women, take fixed positions on his compass of Jews, WASPs, Negroes and Indians.

distinguishing us from other land animals, who show no discernible inclination to *understand* their sexes. There are stereotyped conceptions of animals, as of Jews and of women, but these conceptions are not supposed to exist in the minds of the animals themselves. A rabbit, unlike a woman, does not know its own reputation either for timidity or fecundity. Instead, the preference of most animals, if they are allowed to pursue it, seems to be for thoughtless sexual agreement* or complete separation, depending only upon the season. The attempt of the sexes, in the intervals between copulation, to study each other is human, and accounts in turn for the singular capacity of human beings to experience attraction and animosity simultaneously. This cannot be considered their fault. They are the only mammals, with the exception of white mice, whose mating season is not defined,† and therefore they are obliged to study each other (as mice are not) even as they are attracted to each other. If they were perfect beings, this study would intensify the

* I do not mean to suggest that periods of agreement among animals are necessarily shorter than those among human beings, or more brutal. Animal forms of courtship are studiously observed: male penguins, for example, bring gifts of pebbles (preferably red ones) and execute an awkward but (one must assume) suggestive dance. Penguins also show a rudimentary fidelity. Often the same couples will find each other year after year, in the midst of the large, unruly and raucous crowd which regularly gathers. (See Susan Michelmore, *Sex*, London, Pan Books, 1964.)

† It is, evidently, for this reason that white mice also commit rape. Cf. the mouse riddle in Dryden's *Riddles and Rounds*:

> *Before you mock my timorous shape*
> *Remark my wee penchant for rape.*

bliss, or perhaps the boredom, of their encounters. As they are, study makes it possible, as it is not possible for animals, for the one sex to disapprove of the other sex with which it must join.* In fact, this obligation works almost invariably against enjoyment of the study. The profound trial of having always not only to deal with, but to think about, those who are different from themselves, combining with the elusive nature of this difference, produces a large body of opinions which, if it is no more precise, is certainly more irritable than other bodies of opinion.

These opinions swarm particularly about the topic of femininity. Quantity here, as elsewhere, suggests the strength of the proleptic impulse: the desire to prove is abundant even when proof is not. But this form of wealth, like most other forms, is on the whole a comfort. Capacity for belief, at least in mundane matters, is limited, and it is impossible for women to believe so much about themselves. If they were to believe that all opinions about them are true, they would also have to believe that there is too much truth, a conclusion to which experience in all other situations does not lead either

---

* Homosexuals are, of course, relieved of this necessity, but to judge from their printed opinions, some are not relieved of a similar, and seemingly still more intense, animosity.

The exception is Oscar Wilde, who was incapable of animosity, even toward women. He could bring himself only to be witty at their light expense. Mrs. Radcliffe, "who introduced the romantic novel, and has consequently much to answer for." And "the admirable Mrs. Chapone, whose Ode to Solitude always fills me with the wildest passion for society." And Mrs. E. B. Browning: "In philosophy she was a Platonist, in politics an Opportunist."

men or women. In fact, the increasing presence of women in the audience which receives these opinions, and the palpable incredulity which their presence projects,* seems already to have impeded somewhat the flow of the same opinions in the past—imposing at least some caution or some covering of tracks. It is perhaps for this reason that the opinions have now, for the most part, retreated into fiction, the conventional sanctuary of impeachable utterance.

A second impediment to belief is the element of contradiction which is inescapably felt in any set of these characterizations. It is not easy for a person to suppose, for example, that she is at once conservative and extravagant, or at once pious and materialistic. No doubt some eager ingenuity could provide the needed links—perhaps the pious woman counts up her sacraments and sins and indulgences and penances like so much loose change of different denominations. But the final efficacy of this labor is doubtful, and it is at any rate the job of those who have promulgated the incongruity. As John Stuart Mill argued in a similar context (under that fine, stout Victorian title, *On the Subjection of*

---

* A general levelling of education is in their favor: women know a bit more, and men a bit less. For example, Chaucer had this trick available for his cock Chaunticleer to play on Pertelote:

> In principio,
> Mulier est hominis confusio,
> *Madame, the sentence of this Latin is,*
> *'Womman is mannes joye and al his blis. . . .*

The erudite thing doesn't work any more: women still don't know Latin but now men don't either.

Women), the burden of proof lies with the affirmative. For myself, I am less concerned at the moment with the self-evident disarray of these pronouncements than with certain consistent patterns underlying them.

In the stereotypes which follow, a repeated association of women is with nature and of men with art. In fact, this familiar sexual conception accounts for several of the most amiable stereotypes. As long as the two basic equations can be kept quite clear of each other, good will can prevail. Even if art is considered superior to nature, nature in its place is an agreeable phenomenon. Men may be wheat but, as the Wife of Bath noticed, even the Apostles fed well on barley. And then, nature sometimes not only supplements but charms art. Self-consciousness, the advantage of which people are ordinarily vain, seems occasionally burdensome; and they then admire and envy what seems instead the natural, physical and oblivious being of others—of animals, of children, of women and, often in American society, of Negroes. From this point of view, no revelations have been less welcome in the twentieth century than those of the complexity of Negroes (to white supremacists) and of the complexity of children (to parents, supremacists by age). The mind, Valéry felt, constantly tries to prevent or combat the person's sheer being. Others, then, who seem to the person less mindful than himself, seem also to live more easily, happily, effortlessly. *Being,* Valéry's Monsieur Teste calls Madame Teste, instead of Emilie. And as childbirth (to those incapable of it) seems the most natural and least self-con-

61

scious of human experiences,* it is particularly the capacity to which the praise of feminine being is attached.

The celebration of thoughtless achievement is, nonetheless, subject to at least two qualifications. The first is made when the observer reconsiders his own condition and, experiencing a revived gratification on its account, finds the same supposed thoughtlessness of others contemptibly naive. Or artless, and in that sense not comparable to designed and directed achievements. At this juncture, very often, careful differences, instead of similarities, will be described between the production of the child and the production, say, of rhymed verse. A useful example of the workings of this much argued issue occurs incidentally in an article by Milton Himmelfarb:

> A few years back I read a neo-feminist's approving review of another neo-feminist's book. The reviewer said she agreed with the author that for a woman, a career is more creative than being a mother. That puzzled me: without having given much thought to it, I had assumed that about the closest the human race can get to creation is when a woman bears a child, nurtures him, and cares for him. A little later I was looking

---

* It would be valuable to have a psychological study of women's states of *mind* in childbirth. The lapsing of ordinary interests, observations and criticisms is, one suspects, commonly exaggerated. A woman has been known, for example, to suffer acute embarrassment throughout her delivery because her hair is up in curlers. Moreover, while the recollection of pain fades quickly, what is *said* during the delivery is remembered. I myself recall a shoppy discussion of various antiseptics, and I have known women who could mimic the manners and the remarks of obstetricians years after their children were born.

through the racks in a drugstore and came across a specimen of a common subliterary genre—books for adolescent girls about a young heroine with an interesting/creative job/career. The title of the book was *Phyllis White, TV Secretary*. Then I understood, How can being a mother compare in creativity with being a TV secretary?*

The predictable slur of the neo-feminist reference can be ignored. The phrase *without having given much thought to it* is more interesting. It is precisely with this air of vague benevolence that maternity is always patted on the head—with one hand, while TV secretaries are cuffed with the other. The confusion of sexual function and personal worth seems inevitably to coarsen judgment and restrict choice: the same intellectual vulgarity that brushes off the little Phyllis Whites expands easily to snigger at the unmarried or the impotent and, particularly in the United States, to persecute the homosexual. At the same time, this idealization of childbirth obscures the distinction between involuntary and voluntary achievement which we depend upon in describing any achievement as *creative*. When, as for Indian women, the sequence of conception, birth and starvation is invariable, this distinction remains clear; and the creative act (at once voluntary and socially beneficial) is to procure the means of birth control. But even in middle-class American society, does anyone seriously believe that women, in giving birth, get "the closest the human race can get to creation"?

* Milton Himmelfarb, "Varieties of Jewish Experience," *Commentary*, July 1967, p. 59.

Closer than Bach, whose wives between them produced twenty children? When we think of our primary metaphor of creation, God's creation of the world, we think of the world as an idea in His head (not as a foetus in His belly) and of His deliberately choosing to bring this idea into existence. That is, our concept of creation is profoundly intellectual and self-directed. Adam is formed out of dust, Eve out of Adam's rib: God plays the first sculptor and the first surgeon, He begins Art and Science. In the same way, Vladimir Nabokov speaks of the creation of the novel as a blasphemy, a small but insolent ambition for divinity.

There are, of course, reasons for women to value pregnancy and childbirth, but they are, I think, slowly persuaded to befuddle the issue (in every sense) with creativity. Women may want to be involved in a particular physiological process for nine months: some enjoy the process itself and most rejoice in its conclusion. But not on the grounds of creativity. The astonishment of childbirth is the unimaginable result of having done no more than indulge the body in a prolonged vagary of its own design. And even this detached impression of *uterine* accomplishment is brief: almost at once, the child appears always to have been a separate and complete being, whose body cannot be seen as the product of cellular multiplication. In this sense, prenatal development is *known* but not *believed*. A hubris of childbirth is the opposite, a moral conviction beyond natural verification. It marks an extraordinary schism between the self and the body in which the self acquires conscious pride in the unconscious workings of its container.

Another common deterrent to full enthusiasm in the contemplation of feminine "being" itself denies any such primitive purity in this form of being. It is generally suspected that women infect their nature, not with art but with artifice. They appear, after all, to partake of at least a bastard self-consciousness, which leads them into contrived postures, deceptions and pretenses. These are thought of as almost ineradicable blemishes upon a fundamental artlessness, and it is sometimes indicated that one of the beauties of the primary natural function, childbirth, is its temporary restoration of utter artlessness. At the moment that the child's head emerges from the vagina, it is possible for everyone to *trust* a woman. So Freud, on the day of his first child's birth, wrote his wife's mother:

> I have never seen her so magnificent in her simplicity and goodness as on this critical occasion, which after all doesn't permit any pretenses.*

A second consistent quality of feminine stereotypes is the repeated effort to move women in two directions away from a premised, though indefinable, human center. These movements, like those of an autistic child, perhaps signify no more than obsessive attention to a single subject. But they result in an odd effect of hoisting up or lowering down, as elevators move from the basement to the roof and back again, all day long, or as pieces of clothing, once they are bought, must steadily alternate between being dirtied and cleaned. In this sense, opinions of women reflect two volatile

* *The Letters of Sigmund Freud*, p. 224.

impulses, to set things apart by distinction but also to return them—and then to less than even the common stock. An ideal seems formulated only to be regretted or begrudged, as every feminine virtue implies a feminine vice (chastity and frigidity, intuition and irrationality, motherhood and domination). It was Emerson's impression that this form of volatility was especially prominent in American life—to the extent, as he suggested, that election to office in the United States might be looked upon as a man's most reliable guarantee of impeachment.

Perhaps the most extreme range, between elevation and descent, in feminine stereotypes lies between a statement like Addison's:

> Women in their nature are much more gay and joyous than men; whether it be that their blood is more refined, their fibres more delicate, and their animal spirits more light; vivacity is the gift of women, gravity that of men.

And the Marquis de Sade's observation:

> . . . I believe that the flesh of women, as the flesh of all female animals, is necessarily very inferior to that of the male species.*

All that links the two is the unlikelihood of ever proving either one. Sade, of course, seems extraordinarily rude: one does not want to be eaten, but being eaten, one does not

* From "Juliette" in *The Marquis de Sade* (An Essay by Simone de Beauvoir and Selections from His Writing, Chosen by Paul Dinnage), (London, John Calder, 1962), p. 171.

want to be thought an inferior dish. At the same time, a sentimental exaggeration of virtues, like Addison's, is paid for in an equal exaggeration of defects—usually discovered upon a close examination of the body in which the light and delicate spirit resides. It was, after all, Addison's contemporary, Swift, who focussed for horror upon the Brobdingnagian nurse's breast (rather than, say, the Brobdingnagian butler's buttocks) and who asked that portentous question, Does Celia shit? (Yes, competently. Hence her gayety, her vivacity, her refined blood.) Just as on the same seesaw principle, all sexual diseases are named for Venus. It is really this effect of alternation, the sheer coexistence of irreconcilable opinions, which breeds dissent. The impression is not one of definition so much as of the subject's being tossed up and down in a sport called Definition.

The directions of movement are not, however, entirely erratic. They involve at least two fixed moral judgments. The first is that women unfortunately *are* women, and that their ideal condition is attained by rising above themselves. When his sister-in-law, Mary Hogarth, died at seventeen, Dickens praised her character:

> She had not a single fault, and was in life almost as far above the foibles and vanity of her sex and age as she is now in Heaven.*

On the other hand, men are not men without effort, and their ideal condition is attained by their *becoming*, and

* *Letters of Charles Dickens,* edited by Madeline House and Graham Storey (Oxford, Clarendon Press, 1965), p. 263.

(with luck) remaining, simply men. It is by this route that a perverse appetite for unpleasant experiences, at least in the lives of *others*, develops: various regimens (sleeping in a wet sleeping bag, going to a military academy, etc.) are commonly said to "make a man" out of a man. But copulation too, of course, presumably has this goal, among others. In *My Secret Life*, for example, at the conclusion of an abysmal first performance (which involves the kindest and most patient cook in London at the time), the protagonist crows, "Now I am a man!" It is an index of grimness still at work, however, that copulation is the only shared, innocuous and more entertaining than competitive experience which is felt to have the desired effect of virilism.

These two variant conditions of ideal can perhaps be clarified by diagram:

Super-sexual IDEAL

⇧

WOMEN = **DEFECT**   **MEN** = **IDEAL**

⇧

Sub-sexual DEFECT

A third consistent pattern is that of complementary qualities. This is perhaps the pattern toward which everyone can feel some cordiality, since it shows an understandable desire for sexual order as well as a pretty confidence that balance and economy actually prevail. The feeling is that there must not, cannot, be waste by duplication, that the complementary nature of the male and female reproductive systems must have intellectual and emotional parallels. Ideally, from this point of view, men should have ears (to hear lectures with) and women eyes (to see trinkets with), in which case eyes would be sufficiently defined as "those organs which, unlike ears, cannot take in sound." One might in that way avoid the disturbing sense of overlapping and disorder which, as things are, must constantly be warded off by assertions to the contrary. For example, Otto Weininger established, at least to his own satisfaction (in 1904), that blood transfusions should be carried out only within each sex: since all cells of the female body were female, their being set free in the individual male system, as in all social systems, would cause an immediate internecion. The complementary impulse seems particularly strong in those, like Weininger, whose chief sources of anxiety are mobility, diversity, fluctuation—Keats's "negative capability" of the poet. Such anxiety must urge a uniform commitment to fixed characteristics, an insistence upon the tidy and immutable properties of a reality which, as Bertrand Russell has said, suggests to others only the "higgledy-piggledy":

> I think the universe is all spots and jumps, without unity, without continuity, without coherence or orderliness or any of the other properties that governesses love. The external world may be an illusion, but if it exists, it consists of events, short, small, and haphazard. Order, unity, and continuity are human inventions, just as are catalogues and encyclopaedias.*

* Bertrand Russell, *The Scientific Outlook* (New York, W. W. Norton, 1931), pp. 94–95. Russell assigns the appetite for order to clergymen and journalists as well—i.e., to the sanctimonious on the one hand and

The fourth consistent pattern is related to the third, though its effect is to disturb and confuse what, left to itself, might be the limpidity of the third. In the fourth, women tend to be not merely what men are not, but what the individual speaker is not, and even what he is not *at any given moment*. In the third pattern, let us say, the man is quite steadily direct and forceful, the woman oblique and fugitive. But in the fourth pattern, the woman's nature may be determined largely by the temperament of the person who describes her. The dispassionate sense, for example, of Defoe's judgment of women seems consistent with the temper of all his observations—upon the plague as upon Moll Flanders. Similarly now, in a novel like Philip Roth's *When She Was Good*, which attempts to describe a vindictive and merciless young woman—stones are brought in to hint that she is *stony*—the basic impression is one of the generally vindictive temper of the novel itself.

And beyond temperament, single and passing moods can govern contrasts. If the first seems at any moment lusty, the second seems prudish: but at another moment, if the first seems moral, the second is sluttish. Even a quality which is invariably ascribed to women, like compliancy, will be a defect in some circumstances, a virtue in others, rather as curly hair is sometimes chic, sometimes not, but always curly.

---

the sensational on the other. Clearly, both states of mind are also prominent in the propagation of feminine stereotypes.

The sense of this erratic direction by mood, in an area formerly governed (with some startling exceptions) by a fairly benevolent certitude, seems now particularly strong. At least since the Second World War, the work of assigning stereotypes, not only to racial groups but to men and women, has of course continued, but in a markedly distressed and even demoralized manner. The more stable sexual stereotypes of, say, the mid-nineteenth century provided some tranquility for those who framed them and perhaps also for some of those who bore them.* A perceptible disturbance has now replaced that calm, in relation to all contrasts but especially in relation to the former contrast of strength and weakness and to its former reconciliation: the tolerable exchange of male protection for female helplessness. Among the varieties of suffering which have always been abundantly available, the suffering of men as protectors of women and children was traditionally considered the most severe, and therefore the most valid proof of sexual superiority. Whatever revision of this point the peaceful society might suggest, the always present threat of war denied. This balance of roles, for which everyone must feel nostalgia, was thrown off by the Second World War, which replaced it with an appalling equality in suffering. In the atomic bombing of Hiroshima and Nagasaki, and in the murder of six million

---

* In *Middlemarch*, for example, George Eliot remarks on Mrs. Garth's hearty endorsement of the "principle of subordination": "On ninety-nine points Mrs. Garth decided, but on the hundredth she was often aware that she would have to perform the singularly difficult task of carrying out her own principle, and to make herself subordinate."

Jewish men, women and children in Europe, in the same manner and for the same cause, without distinctions in age, sex or responsibility (all were equally responsible for being alive and human), the modern concept of mutual vulnerability was established, before which the traditional sexual contrasts of strength and weakness, courage and timidity, authority and subservience became meaningless.

The Japanese of Hiroshima should seem to us to have died like women since many of them died in the light, restless sleep of early morning, and all sleep (like night itself) might be stereotyped as feminine—passive, thoughtless, pacific, unresisting. But within the same daylight, masculine ethic of aggressive action, what is to be said of the European Jews who died awake? It is possible for some critics, like Bruno Bettelheim, to deplore their not countering the aggression of the Nazis with aggression of their own. Some yielded (we must always say *yielded*) to despair, others clung to life on *passive* and *subservient* terms. But it is equally possible to suppose that the ethic itself died at that time, extended into monstrosity by those whose minds and bodies were equipped to kill indiscriminately, and exposed as anachronism by their victims. This ethic collapsed before the modern exigencies which the Jews faced and has not applied convincingly to those which have since prevailed. Starvation, racial injustice and atomic fear are also mutual exigencies to which monosexual responses are irrelevant. It is true that American engagement in warfare has, so far, retained a conventional masculinity (and so President Johnson retains the "our boys" rhetoric of World War I). But this rule would disintegrate before the bombing of American cities, as it has disintegrated in those places which we bomb. American women are still divorced, then, from the personal experience of war which American men are obliged to confer upon the women of other countries. Most soldiers must intend to kill only other soldiers, but their weapons erase distinctions in both sex and age. It is not that Vietnamese women are "neo-feminists." It is not that they refuse protection or prefer napalm to a double standard, but that no one can provide protection for them.

In consequence of such changes, inherited Western stereotypes are weakened, and their continued endorsement is forced to be frantic. When Norman Mailer talks about feisty men and languid women, one touches the past—hardly in the form in which it persists in bourgeois enclaves, but as it drags at a mind attempting to reconcile an acute appreciation of the present with a passionate attachment to a masculine ideal. The difficulty, and perhaps the futility, of such a reconciliation account for Mailer's always thrashing quality. At his best, he has a desperate bravado, a last-standness which becomes a way of extracting some vitality, like clotting blood, from defunct opinions.

Ordinarily, the chief mark of sexual stereotypes is their tedium. As the body comes to sexual adulthood, the mind seems to exchange spontaneity, like a secondary innocence, for conviction. But a surfeit is felt increasingly with set formulations, and a hunger renewed for idiosyncratic and isolated phenomena. Both help to account for the present unsuccess of the realistic novel whose main source of energy has been, and still is, psychosexual comparison and contrast. In turn, the reader recognizes the patterns of distinction, and closes the book. Even various degrees of plausibility within the stereotypes no longer hold an audience for them. Most seem ready to give up the chance (now, at any rate, diminished) of "This is how it is" to avoid the certainty of "This is how they always say it is." The original exhilaration of the chance slides irresistibly, through repetition, into banality.

1. Formlessness

The impression of women's formlessness underlies the familiar, and often most generous, acknowledgement of their superficial form. It is of course a physiological impression, and the sexual analogy is transparent: soft body, soft mind. The flesh of women (as Sade would put it) is less resistant and less muscular than that of men. Pinched, it bruises more easily. And if it is impressionable, the impalpable mind must be not only beyond pinching but beyond form. It cannot maintain even so lax and careless a hold upon itself as the body does. There, in the mind, all is liquid and drowning. Solid ground is masculine, the sea is feminine.

The chief consequence of liquidity is formless utterance: thoughts run out of women. In Molly Bloom's soliloquy, for example, thinking and menstruating are similar and concomitant processes. She can no more govern the first, by sentence structure or punctuation, than she can the second. Since Joyce, in fact, the omission of these civilized impediments has become standard in the representation of feminine thought. Sartre applies the technique to a Lesbian in his short story *Intimacy*, but he is independently clever:

> He loves me, he doesn't love my bowels, if they showed him my appendix in a glass, he wouldn't recognize it, he's always feeling me, but if they put the glass in his hands he wouldn't touch it, he wouldn't think "that's hers," you ought to love all of somebody, the esophagus, the liver, the intestines. Maybe we don't love them because we aren't used to them, if we saw them the way we saw our hands and arms maybe we'd love them; the starfish must love each other better than we do. They stretch out on the beach when there's sunlight and they poke out their stomachs to get the air and everybody can see them; I wonder where we could stick ours out, through the navel.

More often, repetitions of the effect are fairly dismal—for example, the letter written by Elena Esposito in Mailer's *The Deer Park*:

> . . . And then I kept saying to myself that I couldn't die because if I did I would haunt Collie and this began to bother me so much that I had the feeling I had to call him up and tell him not to worry, that I wouldn't do anything to bother him, and I was going to make it a nice quiet sophisticated little call but the moment I heard his voice on the phone I was terrified, I thought I was talking to my doctor or to St. Peter, I don't know what I thought, but I started screaming at him . . .

or the soliloquy forced upon the woman named Doris Hollis in Hemingway's *To Have and Have Not:*

> . . . I wish that luminol would work. Damn Eddie, really. He shouldn't have really gotten so tight. It isn't fair really. No one can help the way they're built but getting tight has nothing to do with that. I suppose I am a bitch all right, but if I lie here now all night and can't sleep I'll go crazy and if I take too much of that damned stuff I'll feel awfully all day tomorrow and then sometimes it won't put you to sleep and anyway I'll be cross and nervous and feel frightful. Oh, well, I might as well. I hate to but what can you do? What can you do but go ahead and do it, even though, even though, even anyway, oh, he *is* sweet, no he isn't, I'm sweet, yes you are, you're lovely, oh, you're so lovely, yes, lovely, and I didn't want to, but I am, now I am really, he *is* sweet, no he's not, he's not even here, I'm here, I'm always here and I'm the one that cannot go away, no, never. . . .

Servile. Like Molly Bloom, this Doris is lying awake in bed. (Beds, as the most amorphous articles of furniture in the house, are favored in the stereotype. Sartre's Lesbian is in bed most of the time too.) And for Molly Bloom's menstruation, Hemingway simply substitutes Doris Hollis's masturbation, rather as he substitutes his malice for Joyce's good temper. And yet even with so fine a model to follow, Hemingway remains implausible. Quite ludicrously, the character's phrases, even in her most private circumstances, are trapped in the unmistakable rhythm of all Hemingway's own phrases.

Joyce's indulgence is more common to the stereotype than Hemingway's attempt to scourge it. Molly Bloom, like Valéry's Madame Emilie Teste, is all warmth and sympathy: one could no more disapprove of their liquidity than disapprove of warm baths. *Oasis*, Madame Teste is sometimes called by her husband—whose mind, according to her priest, is a desert. And Sartre's character, too, is as affectionate and vulnerable as she is witless. Moreover, these swirling and disordered sensibilities will sometimes suddenly manage a small force, either of good sense or of humor. They conform to the masculine conception of women's pocketbooks, ridiculous jumbles of things (as Madame Teste, when she is not *Oasis*, is apt to be *Thing*) out of which, to everyone's surprise and pleasure, the owners sometimes fish up exactly what is needed—a throat lozenge, a safety pin, a telephone number.

In criticism, however, the same stereotype is almost always employed pejoratively. It persists there, but as a defect. The critic himself is presently possessed by crystalline purposes of precision, clarity and firmness. Arnold's notion that the critic should "undulate" with whatever work he considers is quite *démodé*. It can be contrasted, for example, with Norman Podhoretz's remark that the book reviewer properly receives new books with suspicion. One does not wish to undulate with suspects or, for that matter, approve of their undulating by themselves. Consequently, a distaste for any indication of temperamental yielding or accommodation is often raised to the level of critical premise: writers must show firmness, resistance, inflexibility. It is on this premise, out of all conceivable premises, that we are told, by Baruch Hochman in *Commentary*, that Kafka is a better writer than S. Y. Agnon:

> Within the psychic smog of Kafka's world there is a tensed, even compulsive will to be, to achieve, to escape. Kafka's obsession with his father, with authority in general, is unpleasant in its clinical baldness, but out of it there seems to grow a tenacity of will, and a counter-fixity of guilt. Such tension is largely absent in Agnon. In psychological terms, his characters are obsessed not with the father, but with the mother, and the result is a propensity to undergo life in a labile, feminine mode.*

The certainty here of the mode in which experience should be met, and the unqualified insistence upon fixities, are characteristic of the stereotypal imagination. The parental influences pop in and out like Fair and Cloudy, Tenacious and Labile, on what Mr. Hochman would probably call a psychic barometer.

2. Passivity

But to return to the flies, I like to think of those that hatch out at the beginning of winter, within

* Baruch Hochman, "Agnon's Quest," *Commentary*, December 1966, p. 50.

doors, and die shortly after. You see them crawling
and fluttering in the warm corners, puny, sluggish,
torpid, mute.

—Samuel Beckett, *Molloy*

Like formlessness, the stereotype of passivity is strength-
ened by a physiological impression—now of the comparative horizontality, atonality and torpidity of women. However, despite the determinism which physiology must imply,
passivity is not condoned. It is felt that this unavoidable
lethargy should be avoided. Some alternative activity, in des-
ignated areas, has always been recommended. In the Talmud, even the rich wife was to take some part in household
work, for fear of her otherwise falling into promiscuity or
morbidity, the two irregularities (first of the body, then of
the mind) which constitute permanent exceptions to the
rule of passivity.

Preventive exercises, however, have been intricately qualified and are still much debated. There is really only general
agreement that actions of conjugal relevance should be encouraged. And even these actions are felt to be passive, at
least as far as action *can* be passive. Childbirth itself, in the
United States, is so locked in the concept of male "attend-
ance" or "delivery" as to seem paralytic. They disappear,
these women, wrapped in sheets and wheeled on carts, like
(the other) mummies. It is the doctor who emerges, upright,
calm, flecked with blood: "It's a boy." And yet childbirth
will proceed, and even end, according to the pace of feminine muscular contractions whether or not it is attended.

(Customarily, the engaged obstetrician is paid his fee, even though he may be backing out of his garage, a birthlike emergence in itself, at the moment so curiously called *crowning.*) It is in recognition of the incontrovertible energy and initiative shown on these rare occasions by women, that their effort is called *labor.*

In childbirth, passivity is swept, willy-nilly, into activity. But some study has also been given to those situations in which passivity yields voluntarily. One of the most important of these situations was first described by Freud, in his now famous substitution of penis envy for passivity as the central characteristic of the female. And to this first active principle, he subjoined a second and related one of shame. The *active* core of shame had not previously been described. Since shame prompts hiding and since, once hidden, the shamed person is supposed to lapse into immobility, the energy of the emotion had escaped all but Freud's notice. But as he explained, nature itself was first embarrassed by the genital deficiency of the female, and devised her pubic hair as a means of hiding it.* Then women, capable at least of taking a hint, invented weaving as a means of hiding themselves still more effectively. This is, again, a more moral than visual opinion of women, a mole's view of Givenchy, but it is undeniably an affirmation of feminine industry.

It is even one of the happier affirmations. Generally, the

* The purpose of male pubic hair was not, to my knowledge, explained by Freud. Some other students of the subject, however, have suggested a visual *emphasis* upon the genitalia, of both the sufficient and deficient orders.

motives which are acknowledged to bring about a substitution of activity for passivity are less edifying, or less pathetic, than shame. Bad temper, for example, is known to rouse women from their customary torpor, as is the desire to disturb someone else's torpor. For the purposes of scolding or interruption, the woman is capable of coming quite excessively to life. A character in *The Horrors of Love* by Jean Dutourd remarks upon this metabolic reversal as though it were a norm: "Women love to be occupied, even if the occupation leads nowhere. The inactivity of the male exasperates them." The key words are *even if the occupation leads nowhere:* passivity yields to *senseless* activity. Either senseless or exasperating. It is known that men think best when they are least occupied, when *they* are passive—and habitually, when women become aware of this artful disguise of cogitation, they are seized by the impulse of disruption. It is then that they plunge into aimless but noisy activity, such as vacuuming the rug.

Feminine passivity is closely related to Negro apathy. In both cases, having restricted the participation of the group, the observer finds that inactivity is an innate group characteristic. According to the same sequence of event and interpretation, the person who grieves for the death of his parent or his child should find himself described by others as lugubrious by nature. Women and Negroes are also linked in the stereotypes of frivolity and fecklessness, respectively. The incongruity of these with those of passivity and apathy is the cost of asserting the radical irresponsibility of both groups. That is, the American Negro has appeared in the past to be devoid, shockingly devoid, of energetic and serious concern for those social, political and economic values in which he did not share. But now, when his previous apathy has developed into open resentment, the Negro develops simultaneously a brand-new stereotype, in the making now, of antisocial or insurrectionary violence. Through some Darwinian caprice, innate characteristics of social (rather more than of sexual) groups undergo quite sudden mutations.

3. Instability

At least two reconciliations of this stereotype with that of passivity are possible. (1) Women are divided into two sorts, the passive and the hysterical. (2) Each woman is divided into two moods or responses. But in turn, the distinction between mood and response is important. In a hysterical *response*, the person indicates her connection, nervous but actual, with external event. Sylvia Plath writes her poem "Cut" *after she has cut herself*:

> *What a thrill—*
> *My thumb instead of an onion.*

But in the *mood*, which is the more associated with women, hysteria is generated from within, like a hormone, and little or no connection with external event is acknowledged.

In general, the feminine psyche suggests an extreme internality to others, like that of a ship in a bottle. Sealed off, the psyche undergoes various but obscure glandular changes, which create a semblance of reactions to reality but are in fact oblivious to it. On a similar basis, Freud and Wilhelm Fliess tried, unsuccessfully, to define the significance of the menstrual numbers 23 and 28: surely this arithmetic of the uterus must be the clue to some larger arithmetic of the whole.* So, still, one might easily reconcile passivity and hysteria by menstrual analogy: the being shuffles about for several weeks; then suddenly, senselessly, gathers its energies for an eruption of violent temper.

This alternation is typically employed in Leslie Fiedler's novel, *Back to China*. The husband moves about town all day having experiences, each a little model of authenticity, while the wife sits at home on the living-room sofa slurping down Petri sherry. On his return, she shifts from depressive to manic gear, and makes a deplorable scene. Her disturbance is, as usual, related to the problems of conception.

---

* Though, as Ernest Jones remarks in connection with Fliess, no regular patterns of psychic periodicity have been determined for either sex, the idea is still casually employed in literary criticism. John Weightman, for example, refers to a presumably clear distinction between the *psychological* "receptivity" of "female" homosexuals and the receptivity of women, which is "part of a physiological cycle." In his sexual ethic, acceptance of the male partner ("submission") is less degrading if it is periodically imposed rather than psychologically chosen. ("Black Chivalry," *New York Review of Books*, August 24, 1967, p. 8.)

Years of disappointment account for the sherry, in turn the sherry accounts for a tardy success: a student of her husband's has impregnated her without her being entirely conscious of the effective procedure. Hence, her hysteria: it is merely her way of bringing the news.

In fact, in bringing any sort of news, women bring only these same states of mind. Elizabeth Hardwick disagreed on one occasion with Frederick Crews' estimate of Edmund Wilson: a quintessentially mental entanglement, one would have thought. But Mr. Crews' rebuttal was brief and, he seemed confident, sufficient: in disagreeing with him, Miss Hardwick had been *hysterical*.* Stephen Spender has similarly clarified the mysterious quality of Sylvia Plath's poetry:

One does not think of Clytemnestra as *a hysteric*: one thinks of her as hysterical for very good reasons, against which she *warns*. Sylvia Plath would have agreed with Wilfred Owen that "all a poet can do today is to warn." But being a woman, her warning is more shrill,† penetrating, visionary than Owen's. Owen's came out of the particular circumstances of the trenches, and there is nothing to make us think that if he had not been on the Western Front—the mud and blood into which his nose was rubbed—he would not have warned anyone about anything at all. He would have been a nice chap and a quiet poet. With Sylvia Plath, her femininity is that her hysteria comes completely out of herself, and yet seems about

* *New York Review of Books*, December 23, 1965, pp. 30–31.
† See *shrill*, p. 150.

84

all of us. And she has turned our horrors and our achievements into the same witches' brew.*

A disturbance in Wilfred Owen is generated by appalling observation; in Sylvia Plath, by her nature. If Owen had ever received shock treatment, the treatment itself would have disturbed him. The shock treatment which Sylvia Plath received—

> By the roots of my hair some god got hold of me.
> I sizzled in his blue volts like a desert prophet

is here as nothing: whatever *happened* to her was, it seems, already part of her. The effect of the Second World War upon her mind, then, cannot resemble the effect of the First World War upon Owen's mind. We are to understand that for Sylvia Plath there perhaps need not have been the later war: its concentration camps and crematoria would have been secreted by her own hysteria.

Spender's awe of hysteria, however, is no longer common. The superior range of perception which can in his manner be attributed to instability has been exceptionally attributed to women in the past, but is now almost exclusively attributed to men. The basic change, which Spender's discussion does not indicate, is the eagerness with which the erratic temperament has recently been cultivated. In the past, women monopolized an incapacity for countering

* Stephen Spender, "Warnings from the Grave," *New Republic*, June 18, 1966, p. 26. Cf. The Witch, p. 140.

stress: they succumbed, on the least notice, to swoons, va-
pors, megrims and brain fevers. In the late nineteenth century,
only the precocious Dostoyevsky celebrated the last, as he
also celebrated idiocy, in men. As long as it seemed possible,
to most others, to dominate experience, mental disturbances
quite simply indicated the weakness of the female constitution.

Now, however, such disturbances have become a secondary sexual characteristic of the fictional male, in whom they
suggest the integrity of a constitution which cannot with-
stand the torment of experience. Even the physiological disturbances of the female are rivaled, as the concept of a
male climacteric is the artificial equivalent of the menopause.
Covetously now, novelists seize upon all varieties of neurosis
for the hero. Psychopathology is in: madness is energy, even
if it is expended upon yanking up morning glories or walking
around balcony rims; civilization is lethargy. Women are
obliged to be sane, as though they were not sufficiently
alert to be insane. Or if they are allowed some small share
of abnormalities, these are kept on the slobbering or sluggish
side—the lumpen depression of the wife in Fiedler's novel,
for example, a day-long self-indulgence in contrast to the
husband's lively *angoisse*. There seems, really, to be a serious endorsement at last of what Jane Austen recommended
at fifteen: "Run mad as often as you chuse; but do not
faint." Heroines now shriek or mope or pass out or go black
in the face—they *lose* control. Meanwhile the men, their
sensibilities activated by experience, *go* or *run* mad. A new

and strange field of competition has opened, between muscular and flabby neuroses, and mayhem makes misery look mean. One realizes that Stephen Spender and Robert Lowell, in emphasizing the prophetic efficacy of feminine hysteria, revive an outmoded compliment. Always a nuisance, Cassandra is now a nitwit as well.

4. Confinement

Range is masculine and confinement is feminine.* This natural law, repealed in the late nineteenth century, became then a social axiom instead. The sequence illustrates, in turn, a law of change: when nature ceases to enforce conditions to which the majority are accustomed or even devoted, these conditions are artificially prolonged by both sentiment and argument. Willa Cather, for example—and for reasons I have never understood—found much picturesque charm in the sight of men, and particularly of women, performing heavy labor. When this labor was relieved by the introduction of farm machinery, she resisted its loss (1) by sentimentalizing its beauty and (2) by fulminating against the

* At least in reference to childbirth, however, "confinement" is now obsolete. It was of course only a euphemism there, like the French *accouchement;* still, it is interesting that the English emphasis should have fallen on shutting, rather than lying, in.

techniques which replaced it. I particularly refer readers to the eloquent denunciation of the cream separator in *One of Ours*.

Similarly, in the nineteenth century, massive resources were spent on the continuation of confinement. In contrast to the eighteenth-century imagination of sociability, poise and wit, poetry took on the celebration of feminine inexperience, seclusion, innocence and timidity. Lucy is "the difference" to Wordsworth because she is a nothing to everyone else. Faust is awed by Gretchen's bedroom because it is tiny, tidy, naive. Dickens cuts out his strings of paper dolls (whom bounders are bound to seduce), and apologizes for a delay which will *confine* his house guest to "the Cigars and the Ladies." Freud argues the superiority of his love for Martha Bernays (no one could love her more, "in cold blood," than he) to the intellectual freedom which John Stuart Mill has suggested for her:

> Am I to think of my delicate, sweet girl as a competitor? After all, the encounter could only end by my telling her, as I did seventeen months ago, that I love her, and that I will make every effort to get her out of the competitive role into the quiet, undisturbed activity of my home.*

And at the end of the century, in *The Doll's House*, Ibsen dissects the same two themes of reaction: sentiment and argument, indulgence and insistence, kisses and blame. (1) Torvald comes home and calls for his little squirrel, his little lark. (2) Torvald chides the little featherhead for her little

* *Letters of Sigmund Freud*, p. 76.

homely vices, smuggling sweets and squandering her pocket money.

The narrowness of women is now an abstract sexual judgment; but it is difficult to know, from statement to statement, whether the characteristic is obligatory or chosen, or to be certain in which circumstances it is convenient and in which regrettable. Certainly, as long as it is recommended, it is presumably desirable. And there are small workings still of such practical and specific directives as Rousseau's: it is not important that women do things *well*, they must do them *neatly*. American medicine remains organized on that principle: the doctors try to think well, the nurses work neatly. On the other hand, when full confinement is realized, it is now more depreciated than patronized. The domestic functions which are strenuously urged upon American women who are not yet involved in them are precisely the sources of complaint against the women who are. Many perform these functions too well, and perfection is as risible as imperfection. Italo Svevo on his wife Livia: "She fills her roles one after the other with perfect punctiliousness. I am sure that even as a baby she must have had a certain dignity."* Masculine verve, dash and impulse are missing, the exultation of error. The dishes are not done as Byron would have done them, the order of the house is at once indispensable and unspeakable. And yet women speak of it—keeping house, they speak of housekeeping. Dullards! Even falling

* P. N. Furbank, *Italo Svevo* (London, Secker & Warburg, 1966), p. 45.

off a cliff, the mother thinks, Mother of Three Falls Off Cliff. And drowning, she cannot review her entire life as she should, her concern being entirely confined to the now forever unshaken, unfolded beach towel on the beach.

The Negro organization, the Black Muslims, deliberately cultivates this absorption in domesticity. The women members affect an antique modesty of dress, an exclusive concern with their household duties, a silence and subservience in the presence of men relatives. This mode is designed to counteract previous and opposing stereotypes of Negro femininity—as the novelist Paule Marshall has pointed out, Negro women in America have previously been classified, according to age and figure, as nymphomaniacs or mammies. (White men made use of the first, white women of the second.) It is supposed then that priggish seclusion may provide a new dignity.

Similarly, the Negro husband, emerging from poverty, prides himself upon being able to support his wife and family, in which case the wife need not leave the work in her own house in order to do the work in a white woman's house. And so she exchanges servility for boredom.* In some corner of their minds, the women of the Black Muslim movement too must know they are parodying this most archaic of white stereotypes. If masculine authority, as

* Dr. Robert Coles, in his recent study of the civil-rights movement, *Children in Crisis*, mentions the nostalgia which Southern Negro women feel for their former jobs away from home.

Daniel Moynihan has argued, is an essential element of an orderly structure of power in the United States, why not play at recognition of that authority as a means of seizing a rightful share of that power?

Practicality is a subdivision of confinement: most often, it is noticed when the man's theoretic, artistic or spiritual capacity is at issue. Women are incapable of grasping subtle principles of conduct, large aspirations, bold errors, grand designs. This is a forgivable limitation as long as they shut their mouths and chill the beer. But unfortunately, many tend to form, and then to express, narrow and hostile opinions of masculine projects, and some may even prevent their realization.

Countess Tolstoy made herself thoroughly disagreeable by objecting to her husband's giving his money away to everyone except their children. More innocently (since she had less money to think about), Mrs. James Joyce objected to her husband's waste of paper during his composition of *Stephen Hero*. It was her strong feeling that several more immortal phrases might well be squeezed onto each page. In fact, Joyce's impression was that she found more pleasure and profit in the landlady's hen's laying an egg than in all his inky deposits. But both women at least drew the line at the domestic *use* of works of art. Countess Tolstoy did not stand on the manuscript of *Resurrection* to reach a top shelf. The archetypal error of this sort was committed by the housemaid who started the fire with Carlyle's *The French Revolu-*

*tion.** Also, Haydn's wife is said to have cut up his symphonies for her hair curlers.

In view of so much depressing evidence of wives' taking the short view, one is grateful for Joyce's occasional nonconformity. He threw his own manuscript (of *A Portrait of the Artist*) into the fire, and his *sister* pulled it out again. In gratitude, he bought her a new pair of gloves.

There is hope, but not much. The issue is complicated by the fact that even the wives of imprudent, impoverished and incompetent men, like the wives of geniuses, err on the side of practicality. Hopeless husbands too have dreams, ambitions, plans. Theirs, unlike Haydn's, will come to nothing even with encouragement, but should not for that cold reason be crushed. Wives who crush even abject fantasies are severely punished in novels.

Translated into literary criticism, confinement accounts for the most familiar and reliable of all comments on women novelists. Their experience is narrow, their characters never leave "the bedroom and the salon" (alternate phrasing, "boudoir and parlor"). It is also customary to speak of these rooms as "hermetically sealed." Women are incapable of dealing with such airy spaces as Wall Street or the Pentagon

* It is rumored, however, that it was not the housemaid but Mrs. Harriet Hardy Taylor, who, out of devotion to John Stuart Mill, burned the *Revolution*. In that event, the fault is passionate rather than practical, and the stereotype shifts to Instability (p. 82).

or the Maginot Line. In this context, Marianne Moore's knowledgeable enthusiasm for baseball is a service to the sex.

5. *Piety*

To prove this stereotype, religions must work like washing machines: men construct them and women run them. To found a religion is inventive, but to keep its rules is pious.

At first glance, this piety seems at odds with the still stronger association of women with deceit. But the two are easily reconciled by an intermediary hypocrisy: it can be assumed that piety, like the courage of animals, is fiercely displayed without being truly felt. Henry Miller, for one, has functioned as an authority on this division between women's professed and actual purposes. His protagonists take particular pleasure in sexual engagements with women who never cease to describe their sectarian chastity. So we are taught that impatience is honest and compunction pretentious.

At any rate, the incongruity of deceit and piety represents only another of the necessary sacrifices of logic to contrast. When men are searching for the truth, women are content with lies. But when men are searching for diversion or variety, women counter with their stultifying respect for immediate duty. They represent, then, as at other times, the atrophy of daring. Similarly, in social manners, the healthy vulgarity of men is constricted by the anaemic gentility of women.

One must suppose, then, that given political power, women would impose deplorable restrictions upon freedom. Their relative innocence in the succession of fascistic regimes which have marked the twentieth century is accidental —dependent, really, upon the fact that their own restriction has been an integral part of the systems of Spain, Italy, Germany and now, most recently, Greece. When Schopenhauer singled out the "lady" as "that monster of European civilization and Teutonico-Christian stupidity," he could not foresee that later "Teutonico-Christian" madness which was to reveal her actual insignificance. And now too, when both sexes are threatened by extraordinary conjunctions of power and pietism, when we ourselves impose such a conjunction of forces upon others, such as the Vietnamese, it seems no more than a distraction, like sex itself, to describe the problem in sexual terms. These assume a natural and permanent separation between masculine appetite and feminine piety, while our experience suggests that, primarily, piety is appetite installed in office.

But given a national imagination which is consistently sexual rather than political, it is possible that to bury the stereotype of piety would be to bury most of our fiction as well. We would lose that store of short stories and novels which faithfully and regularly bring to our attention women's especial vulnerability to religious enthusiasm.* In small tragedies, their narrow and illiberal convictions lead directly to their own destruction or to that of their husbands or would-be lovers or parents or children. In more sanguine works, however, the Henry Miller solution is standard: if the woman is nubile, she can be redeemed from piety by copulation.

Young men are in clear and direct communication with their bodies, rather as the poet Charles Olson is supposed to have announced, "I am one with my skin." Only the date at which this fusion occurs is not certain, at least not beyond the fact that it is postadolescent. Obviously, no one can escape the contrary impression, in adolescent boys, of a fresh shock each day in the encounter of these two strangers, the self and the body. Young women, on the other hand, are uniformly and indefinitely beset by rapture. It appears to be the only signal, other than appearance, which they can give to the world both of their virginity and of their readiness to lose it. Young men thereupon volunteer to translate girls, bodily, out of these delusive (and entirely selfish) excitations into the mutual and realistic, if not rational, excitations of intercourse. Consider the Catholic mania of the young Signorina Oliovino in Bernard Malamud's "Still

---

* St. Teresa has been a favorite object of feminine veneration, all the way from George Eliot's *Middlemarch* to Philip Roth's *When She Was Good*. More generally, however, Victorian heroines were seized by evangelical Protestantism; while now the same kind of folly is expressed through Catholicism, both Roman and Eastern Orthodox.

Life," and her now notorious last-sentence cure by the hero: "Pumping slowly, he nailed her to her cross." And the secular or intellectual piety of Mailer's heroine in "The Time of Her Time," who is briefly restored to humanity, from sillinesses like poetry, by Sergius O'Shaughnessy, who accompanies his services with little running quips like "Compliments of T. S. Eliot."

Not that any permanent good is accomplished by these social workers. It is really only a permanent diminution. The effervescent piety of young girls subsides into the dull and inhibitive piety of wives. In fact, this second piety is believed to seize upon all women, wives and spinsters alike, by the age of fifty. So that really, as far as the marriage of free *minds* is concerned, copulation has been futile. It might as well have been an elective, rather than a requirement, since it seems beside the menopausal point. It is apparent, for example, that when the word *enemy* is thrown past Leslie Fiedler, he immediately returns, like a basset, a description of a middle-aged, middle-class woman who uses her membership in some, any, every organization as a means of harassing liberal imaginations. The *femme noire* takes a corporate form, for example, in Fiedler's piece, "On Being Busted at Fifty," which discusses his troubled experiences in Buffalo: this time it is a Women's Club, "an organization of faculty wives and other females variously connected with the State University of New York at Buffalo."* We are told that, after listening to a lecture by Fiedler and (falsely, falsely)

---

* Leslie Fiedler, "On Being Busted at Fifty," *New York Review of Books*, July 13, 1967, p. 8.

plying him with teacakes, these females initiated the criticism which ended in Fiedler's arrest. Everyone must regret this arrest as still another instance of the ignorant harshness of American law enforcement. But as the police abuse persons like Fiedler out of hostility toward what they conceive to be his nature, as a writer and university teacher, he in his equally predictable (though still less harmful) turn must always look for clubwomen under his desk. Stereotype pecks stereotype.

6. Materiality

You ought to see him in these excesses of absence!
His whole appearance changes—and fades! A little
more of this absorption, and I am sure he would
become invisible!

—Paul Valéry, *Monsieur Teste*

Materiality is the favorite statement of feminine alliance with the concrete. It implies, in turn, masculine alliance with the abstract: Monsieur Teste grows "invisible" before his "touchable" wife's eyes.

The woman feeds upon the fatness of things (Richard Howard's "the fatal etcetera of things in a woman's life") which bore or repel the man. He, in turn, asserts his sensory leanness or indifference, particularly his visual indifference: astigmatism becomes a point of honor. A proof like Schopen-

97

hauer's develops by omission: "Women see what is immediately before them better than men can, because they never look at anything else." Then if a person does not see an object, it must follow that he sees something beyond or above the object. Objects must and will persist in presenting themselves, but men may also persist in not seeing them. Looking is low, spineless, degenerative, and women *voyeuses* of the universe.

Inattention is a simultaneous proof of both masculinity and intelligence. Presumably it is possible for poets to be intelligent *and* observant, but then they are commonly reputed to be effete as well—i.e., they succeed in disturbing only half of the set equation. Serious (or prosaic?) intelligence is gauged by the degree of oblivion to its surroundings, as in the cliché of the absent-minded professor. Vacancy, blindness, crossing the street against the light indicate metavisual concentrations. This absence finds a feminine equivalent only in adolescent dreaminess, which foreshadows sexuality in girls, not philosophy.

Grown women, on the other hand, are supposed to be like brain-damaged children, entirely absorbed in indiscriminate sensory impressions. This is understood to account for their persuasion by candy, perfume and flowers, their later occupation with clothing, appliances, furnishings. Conventional men's clothing is abstract, in the sense that its distinctions must be *known* before they can be *seen*. But the intention of women's dress, an intention now shared with members of the hippie cult, is to catch the first quality of natural objects, eccentricity. This is thought to confuse and trouble men. As a result of a *Vogue* inquiry, several years ago, Mrs. Bettina Ballard issued a caution to women:

> Few men really care exactly what a dress or hat is like as long as it does not make the woman they are with look ridiculous and embarrass their male escorts. Most men are bewildered by the eternal feminine question, "Do you like my dress?" or "Do you like my hat?" He probably has never thought of it because he likes the woman and not her clothes. However, if the clothes are so startling that they make her look like something he has not imagined, then he probably has a very violent reaction.*

The passage incidentally illustrates the appetite of women engaged in writing only for women, for what they suppose to be the male point of view. This is the Marya Mannes gambit, the sturdy, no-run, reinforced-heel-and-toe, good-sensical, what-about-*him* approach. So here, admittedly crude observation is indulged as true feeling: "he likes the woman and not her clothes." Male attention is distilled, essential, purposeful. The emblematic sequence in a poem by Lionel Abel: the woman takes hold of a plum as the man takes hold of her breast.

Women's books trail the same materiality, like yards of chiffon, into ideally uncluttered fiction as well. Norman Mailer on Mary McCarthy's *The Group*:

> Everything in the profound materiality of women is given its full stop until the Eggs Benedict and the dress with the white

---

* Bettina Ballard, "Women and Fashion," in *Women, Society and Sex,* edited by Johnson E. Fairchild (New York, Sheridan House, 1952), p. 241.

fichu, the pessary and the whatnot, sit on the line of the narrative like commas and periods, semicolons, italics, and accents. The real interplay of the novel exists between the characters and the objects which surround them until the faces are swimming in a cold lava of anality, which becomes the truest part of her group, her glop, her impacted mass.

A fine polemical bit, though it is not at once clear why, since the world is full of a number of things, they must all be seen as shit. Nor is it altogether clear why the materiality of the novel glides so easily over into the "profound materiality of women." Is it even to Mailer's advantage to confuse his immediate and main issue, the badness of the book, with all that old collateral sexology? For if the materiality of all women is profound, then a novel about them which emphasizes their materiality might be profound as well. But, in fact, the argument is that however profound feminine materiality may be, it is always shallow, women's lives are profoundly shallow. But no, next their lives are deep and terrible, and Mary McCarthy's fault is not diving into the horror, the horror. Then it is all an issue of courage rather than of materiality: the characters hide behind things and the novelist doesn't push the things aside for fear of seeing what the characters are hiding.

Moral concern confirms the existence of the moralist: he is because he judges. All objects outside him imply the opposite: interest in them does not rouse their interest in turn, and their indifference is appalling. Hence, Mailer's rapid transition from materiality to anality: things in themselves suggest death; the higher the value placed upon individual

100

consciousness, the less the desire to acknowledge the constant enclosure of consciousness by the insensate. Therefore the subjective, rather admirably, defy objects: they will not count them. It will not be admitted, by Mailer, that even the bowels move without personal meaning, the sewers reek with messages. In Malamud's *The Fixer*, the mind of the protagonist functions like a defoliant, erasing the multiplicity and diversity of external forms. As the reader looks *outward* with Bok, the world is shrunken into generalizations, summary and predictable. The visible world is nothing. Bok does not see his prison wall, stone by stone, because the wall does not care whether it prevents his escape or not. The indifference of the object is met or matched or held off by the sensory indifference of the person. No object exists until it seems to thrust itself upon Bok as though *it knew him*. Bok must experience a personal effect, like the slap of a whip or the weight of a leg chain, before he sees the instrument, the inanimate form, itself.

As objects are to space, facts are to time. It is consistent that Malamud, in writing on a historical subject, should furnish it with what he calls "imaginative facts." Past events, like present objects, ignore the living mind: in retaliation, the mind erases them both. The present opposite of materiality in the novel is personality, not abstraction. In *The Fixer*, Nietzsche is like nature, brief, reduced.

7. Spirituality

"You see," he said, "I've decided to go back to a number of my boyish tastes. For instance, I took a certain delight in nature when I was young. I can frankly say that I have decided to throw away some of my conventions and ideals and again get a kick out of nature—that is, of course if you are willing to be by my side. It all depends on that."

"Certainly," said Miss Goering, "but what does this involve?"

"It involves," said Arnold's father, "your being a true woman. Sympathetic and willing to defend all that I say and do. At the same time prone to scolding me just a little." He put his ice-cold hand in hers.

"Let's go in," said Miss Goering. "I want to go inside."

—Jane Bowles, *Two Serious Ladies*

The woman appears here to advantage, as the person capable of refining or ennobling the man who is in love with her. This capacity is ancient: it has been attributed to the Western virgin girl at least since the Middle Ages, when it became a formal article in the code of courtly love. It is of course involved as well in the later dogma of the Immaculate Conception, in which all physical qualifications of the ideal are waived.

In most women, however, spirituality is premarital. When, on occasion, it persists after marriage, it tends to be expressed as an alternate of hypersexuality. Attachment to the woman fluctuates then between two opposing images. The actual woman, probably marked by neither extraordinary virtue nor extraordinary vice, becomes capable, in the partner's mind, of just such extremes. Her character varies according to the time at which it is imagined, and is therefore, however contradictory, always appropriate. If marriage is Luther's hospital for sick souls, these women are the malady by night, the nurse by day. A convenient and economical arrangement, threatened only by the relentless intimacy (enemy of dream) of the contract. The more blithely uxorious seem to be those who from the start can ignore the more reality.

Ordinarily, after marriage, spirituality undergoes rapid conversion in two parts. The first is curiously retractive, a folding in upon the self. Immediately upon her sexual induction, the being previously capable of reforming others proceeds to reform itself. Virginity and identity are lost together, like contiguous tissues. While the selfish (i.e., the normal majority) of both sexes spend all their unmarried time in the pursuit of personal happiness, the wife, in the course of intercourse, is released from so mean a compulsion, and rises from the bed dedicated to the happiness of others. This

103

ascension defines her. What *might* be edifying becomes what *is*, and we arrive, for example, at Reinhold Niebuhr descending to *McCall's:*

> Lust is probably more dominant in the male than in the female, because the female has what a great Catholic theologian, Father Martin D'Arcy, calls "anima," using the Jungian word for self-giving love, as against "animus," the imperious, natural and selfish love of the male. For a woman's whole psychic life is a combination of maternal and connubial impulses; while for a male, fatherhood is a kind of avocation.*

The effect, then, of courtship upon the man becomes the effect of marriage upon the woman. And her withdrawal from influence perfectly coincides with its no longer being needed, with the husband's being fixed, like a point in time or a monument, in sufficiency. Desiring his happiness, the wife divines that its source has become the support of his present nature, and has ceased to be the indication of any future improvement.

Alec Waugh, to whom all students of stereotypes are indebted, has recently described a representative wife-as-support. In discussing his deceased brother Evelyn's divorce, Waugh proposed that the first wife, unlike the second, was not equal to the role of Writer's Wife:

> The "he-Evelyn, she-Evelyn,† 'Orphans of the Storm' Idyll" had been one thing; it was quite another to be the wife, com-

* "An Interview with Reinhold Niebuhr," *McCall's,* February 1966, pp. 90–91.

† In this first marriage, since both parties were named Evelyn, they went

panion, confidante, counselor, and bastion of a great man of letters—the role that Laura Herbert was to fill later, so gladly, so proudly, so lovingly, and with so triumphant a success.*

But the happy run of adverbs here disguises a difficulty at the center of the spiritual or supportive ideal. This is the existence of *others*, outside the given marriage. While the ideal suspends judgment in the allegiant wife, it seems to intensify everyone else's criticism. The one relationship of two persons in which oblivion is indulged, and then often contemptuously, is the parent's relationship with the child. Connubial oblivion is applauded only in didactic generalizations, and loses most of its effect when the actual person to whom the wife devotes herself is a lout or a fool. The second Mrs. Evelyn Waugh may be eulogized but Governor Lurleen Wallace was not. And yet, poor sick woman, she only tried to be a good sheep too. With the wrong shepherd: to dedicate oneself to an ignominious person is considered demeaning. Consistently, of course, it should be the noblest dedication of all, the furthest abnegation of personal preference—as the most saintly survivors in Hiroshima urge that the Japanese should love even the United States. But in fact, the private ideal proves sensitive to public opinion. Unless the wife's self-effacement is, in a sense, licensed by the husband's virtue, she might as well resume an identity.

Still, the failure or refusal to efface herself is the more

---

about as "he-Evelyn" and "she-Evelyn," an arrangement to which most marriage counsellors would entirely attribute the divorce.
* Alec Waugh, "My Brother Evelyn," *Atlantic*, June 1967, p. 50.

repeated criticism of the American woman. Not to support is to undermine, and not to be defensive is to be simply offensive. The remarks of sexual columnists indicate that the supportive stance is essential not only in company, where one might expect the barbs of other husbands and other wives to require the most vigilant protection of the one husband's self-esteem, but also in the privacy of the home. It is an index of our social brutality—either of that, or of our columnists' barely disguised skepticism—that they expect all husbands to limp home at night with shattered egos. The children's hour, the advice runs, should give way to the husbands' hour, in which their wives, over the prune whip, put their paragons together again. Once more, the standard is pragmatic. How can you, the counsellors whine, expect these men to go out and succeed tomorrow if you call them failures tonight? Rebuild them, bolster them, help them, like hamsters, to refill their little pouches of confidence. The implied inadequacy, so groping and gullible, is appalling. Alec Waugh again: "One values the women who make one feel better about oneself."

Inspiration is the executive suite of Support. It refines the problem of careful choice among candidates, since all men may be supported but only those with talent can be inspired. The recurrent sense of imbalance in the creation is here acute. Inspiration is a function which very few women, whatever the aptitude of thousands, can hope to perform.

And even when talent appears, women should not openly

demand to activate it. Properly, they are always prepared to inspire, but as needed or upon request. In this sense, the plan of Inspiration is rather like that of Dial-A-Prayer: it would not do for those people, either, to *initiate* the telephoning. Women who foolishly insist upon this high function find themselves plummeting down out of Spirituality into the half-caste stereotype of The Shrew. *Time* Magazine, for example, having heard that Richard Strauss's wife used to shout at him, "Richard, go ahead and compose!" surmised at once that Strauss was, as they catchily put it, "fraupecked."

8. *Irrationality*

IDIOCY

My words in her mind: cold polished stones sinking
through a quagmire.

—Joyce, *Giacomo Joyce*

Various intellectual contrasts assume a previous decapitation: a severance of the male head from the female torso, of hard bony skulls ("cold polished stones") from soft, yielding, moist internal organs ("a quagmire"). At the same time, the head seems to be relieved of cellularity (i.e., released from matter) in that casual figurative sense in which we oppose the words *cerebral* and *visceral*.*

I take the term *idiocy* from Rebecca West, who uses it in the limited sense of the incapacity of women for impersonal thought, particularly in the areas of politics and history. Miss West contrasts idiocy with *lunacy*, the supposed incapacity of men for making immediate and personal sense. The idiot is close, concrete, practical, ignorant. The lunatic is abstract, theoretic, unreal.

It is only momentarily surprising that a woman should argue the idiocy of women. The materials of any characterization lie outside the writer, who judges rather than joins. The person capable of describing idiocy and lunacy cannot herself be confined by either of them. Miss West first observed this generic idiocy in a woman attendant in the hospital in which she, Miss West, was a convalescent.† The contrast is not only between men and women, then, but also between the ignorance of those who bring bedpans and the intelligence of those who merely sit on them reading the London *Times*. It is obvious that this second contrast, especially since it is made in the context of European politics, involves a perilous condescension. For safety's sake, one hesitates to endorse it. There is, after all, a fixed quality to international politics beneath their superficial variations:

* Schopenhauer compared a woman to an organism "which contains a liver but no gall-bladder," but more liberal modern students customarily grant her full viscerality.

† Rebecca West, *Black Lamb and Grey Falcon* (New York, The Viking Press, 1964), Vol. I, p. 3.

they seem always in the end to create a critical need of more and more simple people who are at least capable of caring for the sick and dying.

Recently, the sense of immanent catastrophe tends to redeem idiocy. "A million sleepers turn," Kenneth Rexroth says, "While bombs fall in their dreams." And they dream too that if anything survives, it will be primitive, stubborn, senseless, no more than a stupid refusal *not* to survive. The imagination turns, regrettably, against the lunatic (informed, analytic, articulate) ideal, and idiocy, for all its presumed effeminacy, comes into its own. The contrast so possessed Yeats that he drove it past the conventional "man and woman, the reason and the will" to man as death and woman as life, to an "abyss-seeking desire" (quite like Norman Mailer's) as opposed to "vivid force."

The only present rescue of lunacy is in its fusion with lovable disaster in the fictional cult of absurdity. The absurd hero is now immediately recognizable by his brilliant, and even courageous, blunders. He is sympathetic and generous (marvelous, for example, with children), and incapable of that coldness with which the cerebral mode was formerly associated (as in Yeats's emphasis upon its *lunar* and *transcendent* qualities). But the violent surge of his mind, like the jet of a fountain or an oil well, obliges him to make a sodden mess of all that lies about him. External catastrophe is, in fact, the proof of intellectual and spiritual aspiration.

In these dramas, women are idiots more often by preference than by nature. It is as much through indifference as through brute incomprehension, that they underestimate the importance of their husbands' lucubrations. On the simple level of J. D. Salinger, Seymour Glass's wife ("Miss Spiritual Tramp of 1948") does her nails and talks to her mother on the telephone from Florida, while Seymour is out on the beach talking to a child (but of course) and advancing through deep, sad, secret thoughts to his suicide.* In the case of natural idiocy, however, good and pleasant women have involved themselves, like Ophelias, with minds that they cannot comprehend but by which they must be bruised. It is in the Scheme of Things—neither their fault nor that of the men, but simply the predestined outcome of every collision between the simple and complex, the mundane and the celestial. In Richard Stern's *Stitch*, the behavior of the American husband, as he wanders about Venice, is invariably, determinedly, erratic. He must ruin his marriage, just as we must sympathize with his doing so: both of us know perfectly well that emotional and personal disorder is the set price of philosophical validity. The wife's position is just (in an immediate, though not ultimate, sense), sad and simple. She wanders disconsolately along a canal, her mind drifting between her husband and the price of fish.

INTUITION

Buddy Willard went to Yale, but now I thought of it, what was wrong with him was that he was stupid. Oh, he'd managed to get good marks all

* J. D. Salinger, "A Perfect Day for Bananafish" in *For Esmé—With Love and Squalor*.

110

right, and to have an affair with some awful waitress on the Cape by the name of Gladys, but he didn't have one speck of intuition. Doreen had intuition. Everything she said was like a secret voice speaking straight out of my own bones.

—Sylvia Plath, *The Bell Jar*

In the terms of this convention, Sylvia Plath cannot properly complain of Buddy Willard's not having any intuition. One cannot expect to hear thoughts out of the bones of Yale undergraduates, since that route of perception is entirely feminine. So much is certain. What is debated is whether or not it is desirable that bones should think or, if they persist in thinking, whether or not they should be heard in all thinking societies. A fairly fuzzy exchange, between Harold Nicolson and Lady Astor in the House of Commons, on this subject:

Lady Astor had said that women had never been given any chance to show their capacity in foreign politics. I said that they might not have been *given* chances, but from the days of Helen of Argos to the days of the Noble Lady the member for the Sutton Division of Plymouth they had *taken* chances, and that the results had been disastrous. "You mean mistresses," shouted Lady Astor. I said No, I was thinking of women's virtues and not their frailties. Intuition and sympathy were the two main feminine virtues, and each of these was of little value in diplomacy.*

* Harold Nicolson, *Diaries and Letters: The War Years (1939–1945)* (New York, Atheneum, 1967), Vol. II, p. 285.

The familiar argument blossoms into a final anachronism: the Versailles conception of diplomacy as artful dodging having become *démodé*, intuition and sympathy (in either sex) no longer seem inapplicable to the business.

A more subtle exchange takes place in Valéry's *Monsieur Teste*:

> Then I told Father Mosson that my husband often reminded me of a *mystic without God.* . . .
>
> "What a flash!" said Father, "What flashes of-truth women sometimes derive from the simplicity of their impressions and the uncertainty of their language! . . ."
>
> But at once, and to himself, he replied:
>
> "A mystic without God! Luminous nonsense! . . . It's easily said! . . . False light. . . . A mystic without God, madame, why no movement is conceivable without direction and sense, without finally going somewhere! A mystic without God! . . . Why not a Hippogriff, or a Centaur!"
>
> "Why not a Sphinx, Father?"

The reception of Madame Teste's remark is representative: 1) The source of intuition is found to be the artless simplicity of the feminine mind. It expresses the peculiar acumen of ignorance, the eloquence of the mute. 2) The intuitive remark made by the woman is the plausible explanation of circumstances which have previously puzzled the man. 3) This explanation provokes an immediate and involuntary pleasure which must, on further consideration, be withdrawn. The intuitive remark constitutes an affront to reason, to "direction and sense" because it leaps out of what is known to be a dark and mindless source. It pounces upon circumstances like a cat, a procedure, which, encouraged, must be supposed to depreciate the measured and logical construction of traps.

In the end, the only intuitive perceptions which can be wholly endorsed, and even these perhaps leave a tiny residue of uneasiness, are those which directly and practically benefit the recipient. In that event, the faculty, like fire for a savage, seems no more mysterious than serviceable.

BALLOONISM

Balloonism, the highest mental quirk, is a conception of the woman's mind as light, fragile, drifting and buoyant. In this guise, women are considered capable of pretty ascents, but they must be controlled by masculine Ballast if they are not to blow away. This conception disagrees, of course, with that of the Helpmate or the Support, the woman whom Alec Waugh has described as a Bastion. But Balloons are almost always young and attractive, and conceivably, having lost these advantages, they may then deflate into Helpmates. At any rate, even in youth plain women are not seen as Balloons. So they at least are available as Helpmates from the start, while lively pretty creatures become the charges, the rather agreeable responsibilities, of their husbands.

The Lost Lady, one of the few novels by Willa Cather which are still read, is an illustration of this stereotype—which in turn is growing old-fashioned. The novel might even be defined as a Middle Western reduction of *Emma*

Bovary to Balloonism. The "lady's" beauty and delicacy depend for their proper functioning upon the control of her husband, Captain Forrester. The Captain is well known for this exemplary effect upon all the weak and excitable creatures of his acquaintance:

> When he laid his fleshy, thick-fingered hand upon a frantic horse, an hysterical woman, an Irish workman out for blood, he brought them peace; something they could not resist.

Without the Captain, horses bolt, Irishmen swear, and Mrs. Forrester goes quite to pieces. As a matter of fact, only the Captain's fat-fingered hold on her had ever given Mrs. Forrester even an appearance of wholeness. Something had always been wrong inside, as it appears to have been wrong inside all beautiful Nebraskan women of the time: ". . . Was their brilliance always fed by something coarse and concealed? Was that their secret?" Mrs. Forrester *seems* a delightful person as long as she is faithful to her grandfather surrogate, but she immediately rots under the attentions of men who are not only in good health and of her own age, but of a distinctly lower social status than the Captain.

The stereotype is somewhat obscured by Willa Cather's bluff, middy-blouse suspicions of both sexuality and vulgarity. The Balloon, like the Idiot, puts in a more limpid appearance in Rebecca West's *Black Lamb and Grey Falcon.* Here, on their visit to Yugoslavia in 1937, Miss West and her husband neatly divide their touristical duties. The Ballast thinks sound, solid, careful thoughts. Wherever he goes, his mind carries a knapsack full of precise and irrefutable facts—

the Serbian soybean crop yields of 1932 and 1933, that sort of thing. Eventually, in any company, he gets a Serb or a Croat up against the wall and pummels him with these facts. Meanwhile the Balloon *appreciates*, her working day is given over to piercing perceptions and lightning intuitions. She is swept repeatedly by gusts of admiration: "What a genius you Slavs have!" When, however, it seems possible that some ruin or some goatherd is *not* going to evoke a fervid response from her whole being, she is swept by equal gusts of depression. It is at these times that the stability, good sense and practical resourcefulness of the Ballast are most in order. The Balloon's acknowledgement of his virtues is like the compulsory modesty of astronauts who must always attribute their personal glory to desk work on the ground.

A higher instance. The same stereotype prevailed in Jane Austen's society, and affected her imagination more than any other sexual contrast. *Northanger Abbey* is its most nearly routine execution: the nice silly young girl, given to melodramatic flights of fancy, is restrained by a practical young man. And yet the contrast does not work conventionally. Henry Tilden is a smug messenger boy, forever delivering his neatly wrapped packages of good sense. In the end, it is amusing to be wrong and irksome to be right.

Again, in *Sense and Sensibility*, the contrast is essential to the novel, and yet its course is deviant. Marianne Dashwood is quite Balloon enough, but then so is her admirer, Willoughby, and he is a Cad as well. At the same time, the Ballast is a woman, Marianne's sister Elinor. And Elinor is burdened with the care not only of Marianne but also of her own young man, Edward Ferrars, who is too lumpish to be a Balloon and too stupid to be a Ballast. All of these novels, in fact, have a disruptive faculty for uncovering both men and women who are neither vivacious nor judicious. *Sense and Sensibility* verges as well upon the asexual thesis that fashions of attitude, rather than men and women, project stereotypes. In a mutual sea, waves of exhilaration alternate with troughs of sobriety. How then to predict which sex at which time will prefer cultivated fields to blasted oaks?

In *Emma* too, disturbances occur. The contrast between Emma and Knightley is as much in age as in sex, so that vivacity seems to belong as much to youth as to femininity. For that reason, the endorsement of moral stolidity is still reluctant, qualified by Knightley's pleasure in Emma's defects:

> "I am losing all my bitterness against spoilt children, my dearest Emma. I, who am owing all my happiness to *you*, would it not be horrible ingratitude in me to be severe on them?"

And before them both, to stimulate indulgence of each other, there is Mr. Woodhouse. Feminine caprice and masculine sense yield simply to time: in both sexes, vivacity is succeeded by judgment, and judgment by senility.

In *Emma* and in *Pride and Prejudice*, lightness is less "sensibility" than intellectual quickness. Both novels contrast quickness and moral consideration as two uses of the mind which are not yet mutually exclusive or irreconcilable. The premised conflict of moral defects, pride and prejudice is incidental to a wit which suspends concern with principles.

116

Perversely, lightness assumes the control of weight: as Darcy's wife, Elizabeth Bennett will teach him to laugh.

In *Mansfield Park*, wit is assigned for the first time only to the left, to those sibling sinners, Henry and Mary Crawford. Liveliness is linked, as it was in *Pride and Prejudice*, with gregarious persons, but now sociability itself has become suspect. What was vivacity has become immorality, and what was Darcy's excessive sobriety has become virtue. These judgments are foregone: the fuss is not only between wit and morality, but also between two embodiments of morality, Fanny Price and her uncle Bertram. The two of them are like Ballasts at war. We arrive at an almost ill-natured determination to prove that women are better disciplinarians than men. The irresolute Balloon, if anyone, is Edmund Bertram—waterlogged at that, and heaved heavily back and forth between Fanny and Mary Crawford. The only mitigation of this moral dreariness is Fanny's valid loneliness. Her virtue would be intolerable were it not for her obscurity and timidity, for her missing as much as despising gayety.

In *Persuasion*, too, the gregarious are at fault, but now they have become silly as well. The former girl wits have degenerated into fools falling off rocks at the seaside, spilling what few brains they were born with. Intelligence is quiet and withdrawn in Anne Elliott, a person subdued by years of disappointment. Unlike Fanny Price, however, Anne Elliott is never insufferable, she will not lecture. An occasional acidic contempt for stupidity runs inside her, but it is not spoken. Instead, and significantly, others have spoken *to her* and "persuaded" her to respect their careful principles rather than her own impulses. Her silence intensifies that sensation in *Mansfield Park* of loss, of exclusion from brightness.

The rights of youth, wit and inconsequence are relinquished in these last novels. Feminine "perfection" is cowed in *Persuasion*, reduced to a "just medium of fortitude and gentleness." The volatile and engaging are now the young men, the Frank Churchills and Henry Crawfords; and nothing is left, in separation from their world, but to doubt their reliability. The last novels become "male" in the stereotyped sense that they argue suspicion of whatever seems more attractive than dutiful. Only at the very end, there is an echo of the earlier supremacy of wit. Frederick Wentworth, reconciled with Anne Elliott, briefly mocks male pieties:

> "I have been used to the gratification of believing myself to earn every blessing that I enjoyed. I have valued myself on honourable toils and just rewards. Like other great men under reverses," he added with a smile, "I must endeavour to subdue my mind to my fortune. I must learn to brook being happier than I deserve."

Anne Elliott herself has long since surrendered, admitted that liveliness loses. The most to be hoped in her situation is that the Ballast itself will, on festive occasions, play the Balloon.

9. Compliancy

THE STUDENT

The publication of Sheila Graham's *College of One*, in which she describes her instruction by F. Scott Fitzgerald, provoked among reviewers a short, happy celebration of this stereotype, which has been in the past one of the most amiable of set relationships between men and women. Francis Coughlin in the *Chicago Tribune*:

> A man in love is, perhaps, the most devoted of teachers, a woman in love the most devoted of students.

And Morley Callaghan:

> Miss Graham's desire to get an education from the man she loved was obviously part of a more ancient yearning—a woman's desire to share her lover's inner life.

However much arithmetic is actually taught or learned, the relationship is unquestionably pleasant. Many marry in its course, which is then its conclusion. For the foundation of the stereotype is premarital or extramarital: the man's "inner life" is a privilege to share (especially if the man is Fitzgerald), but such unilinear pleasures are necessarily brief and irregular. In marriage, the steady accumulation of time threatens mutuality. At any moment, the *two* inner lives may intersect, and John Donnes find themselves thinking the mild thoughts of Ann Donnes. To retain its charm, in fact, the stereotype depends upon even the unmarried woman's keeping her mind pretty much to herself. It is necessary to resort once again to guile, the endemic reluctance of women to speak openly even on academic subjects.

Still, while and if it lasts, there is no guise in which women please more—perhaps it is the only *intellectual* guise in which they please at all. A singular felicity is envisaged, an interchange modelled upon that of experience and naiveté in ideal erotic circumstances. Pornographic couples flourish in a similar ambiance of class hours, recitations, recesses. In *My Life and Loves*, Frank Harris is all avuncular lubricity, the benign bedmaster. Wherever he teaches, the women graduate with Dear-Frank valedictories, expressing their eternal indebtedness for their new knowledge. Similarly, in the Victorian autobiography, *My Secret Life*, the induction of twelve-year-olds is particularly patient and expository. In cases of incest too, the most frequent excuse of fathers is their daughters' having needed sexual instruction.

In his "Story of The Nice Old Man and The Pretty Girl," Italo Svevo has shown that pedagogy may ease even the distresses of senility. At first, the old man lectures the young girl, in bed, on the evils of promiscuity. But later, when his angina forbids him physical exertion, he makes do with writing out his lectures. It is no longer necessary even to see the girl. The treatise on morality, when it is finished, will reach her through the mails. The benefits of this relationship for the pretty pupil lie, according to Svevo, in her original access to food and money. But this is only another instance of Svevo's sexual irreverence. The British professor, John Weightman, for example, could have explained to Svevo that no woman, even in Trieste, can come to rest until she has found her Super Brain, that even her taste for the Instinctive Brute is less compelling.* With such a conception of feminine needs, British professors can come to rest in turn.

I hated coming downstairs sweaty-handed and curious every Saturday night and having some senior introduce me to her aunt's best friend's son and finding some pale, mushroomy fellow with protruding ears or buck teeth or a bad leg. I didn't think I deserved it. After all, I wasn't crippled in any way, I just studied too hard, I didn't know when to stop.
                              —Sylvia Plath, *The Bell Jar*

The student is presently in a sour phase. Pedagogy has lost much of its Victorian good nature even in recent pornography. The teachers in *Candy* pretend to be frowning and severe, and in the *Story of O* instructions have shifted into orders, which in turn are aimed at a sexual humiliation which would have displeased Frank Harris—dispenser of high

* John Weightman, "The Stories Women Tell," *Harper's*, November 1965, p. 166.

marks and leather-bound prize dildoes. Erotic students in turn have grown delinquent, rude and slow to learn—underachievers to a woman.

Moreover, the pacific intellectual relationship proves to have depended upon many silent qualifications. It was essential that the students prefer the teacher to the subject, that they actually do as Schopenhauer said—pick up a book only as a means of picking up its owner. In that event, they would recognize the importance, too, of neither challenging nor surpassing the teacher. At least, not until they are engaged. Freud writes Martha Bernays that, since she is his fiancée, he has "nothing to lose" by her cleverness. But even reassuring himself, he betrays uneasiness. Ideally, students must show a persistent enthusiasm combined with a persistent ignorance. The male Logos loves *Eros*, not that "regrettable accident," according to Jung, the female Logos.

Proficiency breaks the mood, disciplinary problems develop. Fiction swarms with them now—women who have learned the wrong things, or learned more than their teachers, or been caught out in ambition. And even if they are incapable of learning, a condition which in itself might rouse compassion, they still tease and annoy their teachers. The wife in Albee's *Who's Afraid* abuses her husband-the-professor. The first girl in Miller's *After the Fall* hands in Quentin-the-mind's paper on Roosevelt to *another* teacher (mental adultery) and bags an A. Avis Fliss in Malamud's *A New Life* is a teacher herself, in the hero's own English department. But the most regrettable of all is the woman-in-authority, overbearing, rule-ridden, sadistic. The nurse in

Ken Kesey's *One Flew Over the Cuckoo's Nest*: the triumph of the mental patients' lives is the day they corner her and rip her uniform to pieces. Their only other pleasure is in the occasional, against-the-rules company of some jolly, ignorant, unskilled girls, who bring us to The Whore.

THE WHORE

The whore has recently been revived as a special variety of Formlessness. Her old sentimental value—the heart of gold, the rude true ore—is modified. Her goodness now is not a surprise or a discovery, contrary to her occupation; it *is* her occupation. Adult fantasies then revise boys' dreams of nameless, cooperative and uncritical women—endearments and legs joined to blurs. In fact, there coincides a little new flurry of adolescent, masturbatory fantasies—in William Styron's *The Confessions of Nat Turner*, in Philip Roth's short story called "Whacking Off," and again in his "Civilization and Its Discontents."

The adult versions are more specific: one woman is chosen, endowed with receptivity. Moral natures now, like minds before, are unpunctuated, unconfined, miraculously spreading like the stains of some moist divinity. The woman Ruth in Pinter's *The Homecoming* is laconic, impassive, indiscriminate. She is prepared to receive even old Max, shoddiest of fathers-in-law. And she is made oddly dominative in her accessibility, she looms over her attendant men like a prize sow over her litter. She is given, like all others of the type, to sibylline remarks:

Look at me. I . . . move my leg. That's all it is. But I wear
. . . underwear . . . which moves with me . . . it . . .
captures your attention. Perhaps you misinterpret. The action
is simple. It's a leg . . . moving. My lips move. Why don't
you restrict . . . your observations to that? Perhaps the fact
that they move is more significant . . . than the words which
come through them. You must bear that . . . possibility . . .
in mind.

The action is simple, the speech is slow—an unnecessary
waste of sound for a concentrated and frugal person. It is
the men who are loquacious, who jangle—not Ruth. She is
calm, certain, as incapable of embarrassment as of refusal.
The men hang on her, they tug at her for attention, the
brother-in-law Joey doesn't want to share her "with a lot of
yobs." But she is past individuality. She sits in the middle of
them like an imperturbable idol, a steam-heated statue. She
rouses to play the gynecocrat, dictating terms and working
conditions to the pimp brother-in-law, Lenny: she'll have to
have *three* rooms (dressing room, rest room, bedroom) and
bath. Her husband is inalterable, preshrunken—a professor
of philosophy who proposes Ruth come home with him to
America and the children: "You can help me with my lectures when we get back. I'd love that." Ridiculous: Ruth has
been released by his family, metamorphosed from helpmate
to whore.

Elena Esposito in Mailer's *The Deer Park*: ignorant, shy,
inept, untidy, and utterly erogenous. Elena is less competent
than Ruth, less calm, more exploited than exploiting. She is

also more burdened by her own sexuality: she carries her talent around like an inoperable tumor, sinking helplessly under its weight into anyone's bed. A poor little good girl designed by nature to be bad. She looks around, vaguely, for legitimate exercise, she tries to be a flamenco dancer, but no one can cope with two professions. Fortunately, Mind pities Sex: the movie director Eitel marries her, out of integrity, masculine conscience.

Jean-Luc Godard's *Vivre Sa Vie:* Like Ruth, the heroine finds herself in prostitution. She is instructed in its first rule: no one can be refused. Again there is a husband and unseen children. Again, as these personal and narrow responsibilities are discarded, a large single responsibility is discovered in impersonal willingness. In a café over coffee, like Ruth over Pinter's coffee, the young woman attains profundity, the significance of sheer movement (cf. Ruth's leg and underwear) : *I lift my arm, I am responsible. I turn my head, I am responsible.* She dies in her trade, being sold by one pimp to another, in a quarrel over her price. So neither she nor Elena Esposito has quite Ruth's invulnerability: one dies, one marries. Ruth governs, the other two obey. Ruth evokes fear, the others pity. But all are beyond judgment. There is no arguing with their predestined whoredom, their nature is fixed, simple, "naked as a nose."

And now the whore filters down to the level of Charles Jackson's *A Second-Hand Life,* the square "nymphomaniac" who eyes even priests, but is really of course always rummaging for an old happiness, a true love lost, a cottage to keep clean. "Accept, and don't expect anything back," she preaches. Be honest, make mistakes, pay for them. A slack under lip, stiff upper. Winnie Grainger is married off (like Elena) in the end, settled down, patched up—it is all unremittingly banal, even to Marya Mannes being sensible and gruff again: "Charles Jackson has had the guts to create a heroine who loves men more than herself and is honest enough to admit it."*

Jackson is a reversion, though. He ascribes romantic motive when the peculiar recent development of the type has involved ditching all previous ascriptions of motive, base or pure, and of reasserting sheer motiveless accessibility: moving because movement is possible, opening orifices, like mouths and vaginas, simply because they *can* open.

Two tastes seem to alternate in time. Imagination veers away from sexual agreement or contract, substituting either fantastic resistance or fantastic acceptance. The first perhaps belongs especially to cultural periods of energy, as Freud emphasizes feminine retreat and masculine force, the dream of rape; the second to languid periods like our own, the dream of total compliance.

THE SERVANT

As people cease to remember ever having been helped, at least around the clock, this pleasant stereotype fades. The sleeping-in servant is caught on the verge of extinction. But in the past, at its most plentiful, the type promised uncritical

* *New York Times Book Review*, August 13, 1967, p. 17.

obedience and respect combined (as these childlike qualities cannot be in children) with sexual maturity.

Perhaps no other concept of women, even the student, has been so entirely satisfactory on all levels of relationship. It was, in the first place, grounded in actual opportunity. The innumerable variations upon the sexual encounters of masters and servants (Pamela, Moll Flanders, Jane Eyre, and all such eloquent struggles of decorum and desire) reflect the historical fact, which Steven Marcus has discussed in *The Other Victorians*, that the woman servant was the primary sexual opportunity of society before the twentieth century. The type was also imaginatively soothing. At least in prospect, no other woman suggested less effort, less resistance, less responsibility. Economic control seemed to guarantee erotic control. And without fuss. In intervals of separation, one might have the calm sense of the servant's making herself useful somewhere else in the house: she would, literally, make the bed she lay in. And for the sadistic, exceptional rights of discipline lay in the relationship of employer and employee. Strindberg recalls, in *Son of a Servant*, a woman servant who, to her own amusement and that of his brothers, uncovered his body as he was lying asleep in bed. Informed of this impudence, he was entitled to whip her. Both to their own diversions.

In the United States, the stereotype found its most satisfying expression, at least in the past, in the Southern Negro woman. Ignominy by race as well as by means, enhanced her as the type. The bald assertion of racial supremacy was, in such encounters, incomparably shaded by the sense of racial impropriety. And the Negro woman's particular availability was matched by the notion, as James Baldwin has described it, of her particular appetite:

> Sometimes, sure, like any other man, he knew that he wanted a little more spice than Grace could give him and he would drive over yonder and pick up a black piece or arrest her, it came to the same thing. . . .*

Ultimately, the white racist converts his opinion of Negro hypersexuality into insult ("animals, nothing but animals"), whereas Baldwin suggests it as praise.

Occasionally, the charms of servility are transferred to the simple wife of the complex husband, as in Madame Teste's remarks on her marriage in Valéry's *Monsieur Teste*:

> Strangely married as I am, I am so with my full knowledge. I knew very well that great souls settle down only by accident; or indeed in order to have a warm room where whatever fraction of woman can come into their scheme of life will always be touchable and kept. It is not distasteful to see the sweet shine of a fairly pure shoulder drawn up between two thoughts! . . . Gentlemen are like that, even the deep ones.

The last sentence is the essential utterance of the tweenie's mind, at once mystified and complacent, accustomed to receive without quite comprehending the sporadic advances of the deep gentlemen of the house. The tweenie is supposed to subsist on physical vanity. Otherwise, she is content to play the "whatever fraction," to squidge in from time to

* From the title story of *Going to Meet the Man*.

time "between two thoughts." How adaptive and unde-
manding, how preferable even, for example, to the Student
who wants to share the two thoughts. The servant is the
kitchen version of all sexual myths involving the human
female and the divine male, the mundane rendering of that
idyllic "gentle acceptance," cowlike and dazed, which is recently revived in Robert Lowell's *Prometheus Bound*—in its
conception of Io's affair with Zeus.

The mundane, if anything, surpasses the mythical, since
it furnishes possibilities of retrospective feelings which the
mythical does not. Male divinities cannot feel guilt, they can
merely move on to other incarnations and other humble
human females. But the servant has been the fictional reservoir
not only of sexual freedom but of an equally rich aftermath
of regret. Which was the more prurient in the nineteenth-
century novel, the seductions themselves or the subsequent
self-recriminations? One thinks of Hardy, above all of Tolstoy and his prolonged indulgence of sexual conscience in
Resurrection. The last employment of the libido.

The uses of the servant, more recently, have had either
to be reordered or abandoned. I should think Joyce's parody,
in one of his letters, of Hardy's *Life's Little Ironies*, his
playing over its sociosexual clichés—the servant wife, her
semiliteracy exposed, blows her nose in her own ill-phrased
letter—might mark the moment of the mode's exhaustion.
But for Joyce it was merely a mode to discard; for others,
it seems to have been a regrettable loss, imposed by external

circumstances. Changes in the conditions of work, of payment and of social independence diminished the old availability of the servant, the old impunity of the master. And without them, there was no longer a foundation for the benevolence toward the servant which had always before finally prevailed. The sexual intersection of economic classes was modified: the woman became the mistress, the man the servant and the theme humiliation. The servant took the advantage, and the reader's vicarious satisfaction was vindictive. The master had previously bent down to the servant, now the "proud and stiff" mistress was *brought* down by the servant—as Lady Chatterley was dominated by her gamekeeper and Miss Julie by her houseboy. (The emphasis upon the polite titles of the women in contrast to their rude copulation is the same in both compositions.) Essentially, if women were not to play servants, others would play servants against them.

The fact that Lady Chatterley is pleased by Mellors does not preclude his disciplinary function. Each of their encounters emphasizes her being forced to relinquish not only decorum but whatever grace of mind or manner had previously made her an individual person as well as a body. A new resentment prevails of what used to be called "airs." The "air" in question is that of a dignity to which the servant never pretended. It is mocked by repeated exposures of women's actual tastes, which are presumably more bestial than men's. Customarily, they disguise these tastes briefly in the company of the protagonist, they pretend a refinement equal to his own. But he is never or not long deceived:

irresistibly, at some point in the relationship the women's natures will revert. The protagonist will find them down at their true level, attended by men who are obviously less perfect than himself. He is then torn between rage and gratification. If the women are out of reach, they are also beneath contempt.

THE MOTHER

What a rest to speak of bicycles and horns. Unfortunately it is not of them I have to speak, but of her who brought me into the world, through the hole in her arse if my memory is correct. First taste of the shit.

—Samuel Beckett, *Molloy*

The Mother is particularly useful as an illustration of *the explosive tendency*: each stereotype has a limit; swelled to it, the stereotype explodes. Its ruin takes two forms: (1) total vulgarization and (2) a reorganization of the advantage, now in fragments, about a new center of disadvantage. In this second form, the same elements which had constituted the previous ideal make up the present anathema.

It is difficult to determine how much of any stereotype arises from insistence or argument, the imposition of a preference. Certainly, statements of the maternal ideal seem to have taken on the explicit and reiterative character of the stereotype in response to increased social questioning of its sufficiency. This effect of pressure is exceptionally clear in an 1883 letter of Freud's in which he discusses his future mother-in-law:

> I do not think I am being unfair to her; I see her as a person of great mental and moral power standing in our midst, capable of high accomplishments, without a trace of the absurd weaknesses of old women, but there is no denying that she is taking a line against us all, like an old man. Because her charm and vitality have lasted so long, she still demands in return her full share of life—not the share of old age—and expects to be the center, the ruler, an end in herself. Every *man* who has grown old honorably wants the same, only in a woman one is not used to it. As a mother she ought to be content to know that her three children are fairly happy, and she ought to sacrifice her wishes to their needs.*

Freud drives to the verge of defining the fundamental conflict of individuality and maternity. It is only in the last sentence that he sets himself against his own immanent definition and supports opinion instead: "She *ought* to be content." The total absorption of the woman into the maternal role was more intensely preferred as it became less actual.

When the imagination insists upon a form in opposition to reality, the effect must perhaps always be one of simplification. Actual variations are ignored in the effort to dream of consistency: "she *ought* to sacrifice her wishes." At the present time, we have advanced to what seems the final vulgarization of the mother, and television furnishes perhaps her

* *The Letters of Sigmund Freud*, p. 38.

132

most blatant images. For example, a program about the FBI, January 22, 1967:

> An exceptionally ugly middle-aged woman is led into the office of the FBI hero (Efrem Zimbalist, Jr.). Her expression at first suggests no more than a liver complaint, but the dialogue quickly establishes that her son is dead. It looks to her like foul play: a policeman is accused of the murder. The mother says she knows her son was a bad boy, but, but—(breakdown, racking sobs, contorted features). Zimbalist, Jr. strokes the left side of his nose with his left thumb. He is embarrassed by the mother's Instability, he would like to get on with the rational business of proving the policeman's innocence.
>
> After several seconds of this noisy stalemate, Zimbalist, Jr. conducts the mother to the door. Through it, he tells an unseen secretary to get Mrs. Distraught a glass of water and a cot to lie down on. The genuine relief which is felt with her departure from the scene constitutes a rare moment of rapport with the FBI. But the point is thought to be still clouded. A second FBI man therefore spells it out: Here was a dreadful son—a junkie, a pimp, a firebug, etc. Yet This Woman, His Mother, Loved Him. Zimbalist, Jr. waggles his head (mystified awe of maternal feeling). The solution of the case gets under way.

At the same time, television commercials have achieved a fusion of Maternity and Materiality. In other contexts, of course, the second is defamatory; in the commercial the two coalesce in a single ideal. Competitive mass production exalts materiality as a feminine virtue, the means of most fully realizing either (1) the beauty of young girls (deodorants, mouth washes, hair sprays and rinses) or (2) the domestic assiduity of wives and mothers (toothpastes, detergents, floor waxes). But since the fundamental commitment is to the detergent rather than to marriage, the program's vulgarization of the stereotype shifts, in the commercial, to its malformation. The climax of the detergent commercial when the woman lunges down into the porcelain womb of the washing machine, to haul out the whitened T-shirts, is more monstrous than sentimental. The grimaces are savage, the gestures obstetrical, maniacal. Quite accidentally, the relationship of dedicated housekeepers to dirt, which converts once carefree virgins into vigilantes, is exposed.

Vulgarization of the stereotype is not of course confined to television. Our punishment for its unconscionable exploitation lies all about us. One might take Jean Stafford's *A Mother in History*, a study of Lee Oswald's mother, as an example. Here is the putrefaction of the dream, the idealcum-maggots. "On Mother's Day, let's come out and say he died in the service of his country." In the outermost regions of sentimentality, the comprehension of cruelty or violence utterly fails. All actions which follow upon, or are in any way associated with, the soft fact (having given birth) seem possible to admire. Entirely framed by her country ("I love my United States") and its common culture, an incarnation of its emphases, Mrs. Oswald looms up and glows before us like a commercial mother, selling her malignant offspring like a plastic food wrap: "I've got some real dynamite and some real exclusives." She and Jean Stafford might "split the proceeds" of "a sort of soap opera."

It will be called Mother's Night, and run just after midnight snacks on weekdays.

That reminds me of the old joke about the female soul. Question, Have women a soul? Answer, Yes. Question, Why? Answer, In order that they may be damned. Very witty.

—Samuel Beckett, *Molloy*

As the stereotyped ideal grows intolerable, reaction against it takes the form of emphasis upon those who misapply it. It is, after all, Freud who described, simultaneously, the duty of the mother to sacrifice herself to the children and her demand that they sacrifice their wishes to her. Properly, she weaves her life about the children, and then in the children's dreams she is a spider (or, for Jung, a serpent or sarcophagus or specter). The more ideal the conception of a human function, the more resentment and suspicion it arouses: we are entirely accustomed, in the consideration of maternity, to this jolting between soul and damnation. We are as familiar with the accusation of consumptive attachment as with the praise of selfless care. In this sense, women are at once the child makers and breakers; no idea is more commonly fixed than that of the filocidal influence of the mother. So we pass now, as it seems by iron logic, from the exhausted generalizations of "Momism" and "womanization" to the specific attribution, by Daniel Moynihan, of the urban Negro's social problems to the domi-

135

nance of the Negro mother. Or to the causes of infantile autism, which being still uncertain are conveniently (if loosely) associated, by Bruno Bettelheim, with maternal deficiencies.* Obviously, it is impossible for women either to give or to withhold attention without risking the injury of their children. The eagerness with which mothers are chosen as the cause of regrettable effects is a psychological fact in itself, an independent fixation, predictable in the discussion of all social problems.

But our distrust of maternity is an innocuous preoccupation in contrast to our resentment of those who do not take part in it. Nothing is more reliable than the irritability of all references to prolonged virginity: behind us, and undoubtedly before us, stretch infinite tracts of abuse of *maiden ladies, old maids, schoolmarms, dried-up spinsters*, etc., etc. Since copulation is presupposed to be pleasurable, this hostility is directed, incomprehensibly, at those who are deprived of pleasure. The insistence, in fact, seems to be upon *uniformity* of pleasure, since resentment of these women is paralleled only by the resentment of homosexual men and women by heterosexual men. But for heterosexual women, the issue is complicated by an insistence upon subsequent and visible *proof* of copulation as well—upon conception, pregnancy and childbirth. Whatever the baleful effects of the mother, it is essential to be one. But of course this means that even the most cooperative of women enjoy, actually, a rather

* See Bruno Bettelheim's *The Empty Fortress* (New York, The Free Press, 1967) and, in disagreement, Clara Claiborne Park's *The Siege* (New York, Harcourt, Brace & World, 1967).

brief period of approval, that portion of their lives in which they are capable of reproduction. Fortunately, this period is now somewhat extended, into childhood, by the recently increased sexual taste for nymphettes, but it is extended into middle age with more difficulty.* Those who are eager for commendation may rid themselves easily enough of the "virginal" defect, but eventually whatever they do is bound to be "menopausal." In the Californian sheet, *Ramparts*, a waitress is a "menopausal waitress."† Even the deposition of a place mat must be instinct with reproductive opportunity.

10. *Two Incorrigible Figures*

THE SHREW

Brigid Brophy has won herself a small reputation in recent years as one of our leading literary shrews.
——*Times Literary Supplement*, June 1, 1967

The present condition of the shrew indicates an obscure, rumbling disturbance of the former stereotype. Perhaps none

---

* Various technological advances affect this issue. With central heating, feminine puberty is supposed to be attained precociously. At the same time, the synthesis of female hormones may, in time, eliminate the menopause. See R. A. Wilson, *Feminine Forever* (New York, M. Evans, 1966).

† *Ramparts*, July 1966, p. 1.

is ever lost, but occasionally one is modified to suit new circumstances—rather as, in more cheerful surroundings, the same dresses are taken in or out to fit different figures.

The most extreme admission of unrest is the creation of a new stereotype. For example, a favorite impression at the moment is that women are uniformly marked by psychic confusion. A publisher's blurb for a recent novel:

> What gives *A Woman of My Age* its special distinction and excitement is Nina Bawden's extraordinary insight into the lively mind and uncertain heart of an attractive, cultivated woman who, while intensely self-aware, feels baffled by the contradictions in her own nature. Elizabeth, in short, is very much a woman of our age.*

A transference seems to have occurred: an increasing uncertainty *about* the Elizabeths is, rather cannily, attributed *to* them. Then at least everyone can be supposed to feel equally uncertain of the subject, as of China or the weather. All mutual inadequacies make for sexual peace.

The alteration of the shrew is less amicable. It shows an increment of certainty rather than of doubt, and of a thoroughly morose certainty. In the past, the unmarried shrew was a challenge, it was a popular sport to tame her. The game amounted to no more than a comic, if brutal, variant of courtship. At one extreme of taste, the lover prostrated himself before the beloved; at the other, he forced the beloved to prostrate herself before him. The marriages resulting

* *New York Times Book Review*, July 16, 1967, p. 22. (Harper & Row.)

from these prostrations seem to have held equal promises of success.

And even the married shrew held an acknowledged and reputable place in the social imagination. An attractive couple, for the marriage jokers, was one like Socrates and Xantippe, the man of great mind who endures a wife of abominable temper. In the Talmud too, a certain scholar never came home without a small gift for his ill-natured wife. Asked why he indulged her fault in this way, the scholar spoke to the virtues of cross women: *They bear our children and keep us from sin.* The execution of physiological duties earned them privileges of temperament. Profiting by the one, a wise man allowed the second.

All such wry contracts have now been broken, and with them their fine vocabulary (*termagant, harridan, virago*) has fallen out of use. The whole matter has turned sharp left into glumness, and glumness in turn breeds abstraction. The old, ludicrous rolling pin on the husband's head advances to his *castration.* The latter is now seen as a daily and entirely domestic occurrence, less dramatic than emptying the ash trays. Nonetheless, it vastly enlarges past resentments and retaliations. The husband's response is not to come home bringing little bribes for tolerance, but to stay away meeting his lawyer or driving through red lights. Ours is pre-eminently a literature of disturbed men in mechanical motion. (Chevrolets, Dodges and Volkswagens predominate.) The drivers return home only for the essential confrontation of the penultimate chapter. Thereafter, separation is irrevocable. The more hollow our social jargon of arbitration grows (saving this marriage, looking at both sides, sitting down at the conference table), the more violent the private imagination of sundering.

THE WITCH

Like the Shrew, the Witch is in present trouble. But the one trouble seems dogged and sober, the second febrile and forced, a whipped-up exasperation. The second has no even plausible object. The preternatural female is extinct, and none of her former manifestations carries conviction now. We have lost:

(1) *The romantic witch.* In the initial phases of attraction, the man was once pleased to call the woman a *sorceress*. A happy gallantry, at once flattering her endowments and explaining his own loss of composure. If she was only human, his passion might seem impressionable. But if she wielded magical powers, then his passion was out of his hands. Descartes himself would have been as helpless in the same circumstances. But even in the past, a lurking distrust of this enchantment usually brought it to an end at the couple's earliest convenience. In Freud's correspondence, for example, a quick transition takes place—from his humble delirium to an insistence upon Martha Bernays' straightness, responsibility, discretion, obedience. The sorceress must prove, after all, to be a good citizen.

Such extravagances of praise, however fleeting, are now felt to be lax. The word *sorceress* itself dwindled down to *vamp* by the twenties, and from that to nothing. The only present romantic extension beyond nature is the *sex symbol*, like poor pawed Marilyn Monroe, and this is too sensual for sorcery.

(2) *The domestic witch.* Traditionally, magic was divided between men and women, exactly as the professions and the trades continue to be divided. Male magic was intellectual, female magic was manual. The men pored over portentous charts and symbols and were visited by high-ranking devils. The women cackled and mixed vile broths in pots. This arrangement was felicitous: the double standard rarely furnishes such lively parts to both performers. But of course neither exciting approach to improper knowledge survived later, and again separate, commitments to science and industry. Some nostalgia, however, is perhaps expressed in the present male executive ambition for *charisma*.

(3) *The physical witch.* Science has undone this manifestation as well. Previously, whatever was different and unexplained seemed also sinister. In such circumstances, the more articulate expressed horror of their opposite. In the West, female genitalia were seldom represented in art, the ideal hermaphrodite had female breasts and male genitalia. In many prescientific cultures, menstruation (Joyce's "the dark shame of womanhood") was reproved by ostracism— on the grounds either of contamination or of preternatural influence. The Talmud mentions the folk belief that if a menstruating woman walks between two men, one of the men will experience some misfortune. Childbirth had similar associations: it too was considered a psychic transformation, an involvement in the ungodly. (How could one believe

that *God* devised such carnage?) In the Talmud, where concern often defies all other directives, one husband plays countermagician himself, stopping up the windows with thorns and tying nails to the legs of the bed, to help his wife's delivery. Instances of women having to be "churched" (purged of impious influence) after childbirth bob up even now—according to the *New Statesman*, Wolverhampton, in England, is still that sort of sexually nervous town.

Elsewhere, this frightened fascination has subsided. Not much is left—a remnant fear of childbirth, a remnant disgust with menstruation. Essentially, technology has reduced these functions by euphemism. The occasionally witnessed birth, in a taxicab or an elevator, stirs excitement; and there are now of course some young husbands who attend the normal, if not the Caesarean, births of their children. Generally, however, the sound-proofed delivery room creates a well-intentioned ostracism of its own. Menstruation in turn is now socially so concealed as to seem more denied than before. It is perhaps this sense of reconstituted taboo which has prompted Doris Lessing, Sylvia Plath and Anne Sexton to violate it.* Their frankness is partly a reaction against the insistent blandness of modern femininity. We are accustomed now to admit only the blood of wounds—the effects of accident, crime and war. The natural bleedings of women

---

* Louis Simpson's ingenious comment on Anne Sexton's last book, *Live or Die*: "A poem titled 'Menstruation at Forty,' was the straw that broke this camel's back." ("New Books of Poems," *Harper's*, August 1967, p. 91.)

remain an indelicacy, while deadly bleeding has become a commonplace.

(4) *The mysterious witch*. The obverse of (3): the incomprehensible attracted as much as it repelled. The Talmudic recommendation for the handling of women and children, "to push away with the left hand and draw them near with the right hand," recognized impulse as well as discipline. The unknown, like a foreign country, haunts the familiar. And from the unknown, the extension to the dark and obscure is irresistible. As the sexual act is covert, the woman in Yeats's early poetry is "the flying darkness," the headless horsewoman. Leslie Fiedler has discussed the persistent association, in nineteenth-century northern novels, between dark hair and mystery, evil and marvellous mystery: Scott's Rebecca, Hawthorne's Miriam. These effortless associations were nonetheless powerful, drawing the light people to the dark, the gentile novelist to the Jewish antiheroine. In *The Second Stone*, Fiedler impudently reverses the stereotypes, to make the brunette blatant, the blonde ineffable.

It is clear that the route of comprehension of the mystery was assumed to be sexual, as Samson came to "know" (or think he knew) the "stranger" Delilah. As sexual intercourse has been seen as the cure of pious extremes in young women, there clung about feminine magic the possibility of exorcism by the same technique. The notion is recently revived by Peter Ustinov in his play, "The Unknown Soldier and His Wife." An Archbishop speaks to the Wife:

. . . The little demons have entered you by your ears. Together we will wrinkle the wicked little fellows out of all the
orifices where they may be hiding.*

But the coy cuteness of the statement gives it away. Slimy
and silly, and not magic at all. There seems to be no further
hope of translating the impulse to control into the duty of
exorcism: the women are no longer possessed and the men
no longer therapeutic. If anything, they themselves now
claim possession, and are wholly engaged in self-exorcism.

What is common to all these extinct versions of witchery
is the imagination of a governance which mitigates fear and
encourages encounter. One has the impression, for instance,
that the punishment of witches in Salem was conducted with
decorum. Knowing what to do, the authorities need not lose
their heads. Whatever the subterranean thrills of the hunt,
the forms of a judicious procedure in the interests of social
security could still obtain. Some witches might be reformed,
the rest could drown.

Such small recreations of the concept as are now put forward lack this confident calm. The hero of *An American
Dream*, Rojack, concluded "a long time ago that all women
were killers," and he feels his wife's slitting of his (spiritual)
throat. In rebuttal, he murders her—but that action too is
neo-spiritual, fantastic. The hatred of the woman is real
enough, but its magical terms seem only the means of exag-
gerating the depth of her evil and the efficacy of Rojack's
good. Sexual encounters with the bewitched have a new

* *Ramparts*, July 1967, p. 33.

ferocity: incapable of exorcism, the hero rushes at abuse. The malign spirit may be insuperable, but at least a few of its bones can be broken. And there is of course the comfort of Cherry-the-one-true-friend, a demonic girl too but a creature possessed for the *good*, like a flealess rabbit's foot, an innocent "Power"—at pinochle.

But Mailer's attraction to witchery seems impersonal, undifferentiated, simply olfactory. His associations are those of the domestic witch, the maleficent cook. His imagination is offended by a combined odor of clam shells, salt marshes, female bodies and sickening brews—"perfumes which leave the turpentine of a witch's curse." Choking with sexual disgust (fresh sheets! fresh air!), he describes a nose's nightmare. The witch herself is dead, Mailer smells her unwashed corpse.

❧ IV ❧

DIFFERENCES IN TONE

◄§ In intellectual matters, there are two distinctions between men and women, though only one of them applies uniformly and consistently to all participants. This is the first distinction, which is simple, sensuous and insignificant: the male body lends credence to assertions, while the female takes it away. Once in a while, by an exceptional solidity (like that, say, of Gertrude Stein) the female body overcomes this disadvantage. Ordinarily, however, manful effects are a strategic error for the woman, tending to replace a meager intimidation of the audience by their ample amusement or even hostility.

Obviously, male figures vary as much as female figures. They are mutually affected by such problems as thick ankles, short necks, fat thighs, bellies and paunches. Male figures do not, however, *seem* to vary as much (or as disastrously) as female figures: for one thing, conventional modern male clothing is more evasive than conventional female clothing. While tailors, then, may be beyond this visual deception and so skeptical of all human statements, other people are inclined (it is only a tendency) to take what men say seriously. The subliminal assumption is that from weight must come weight: men's shoes alone seem a promise of truth. This effect is heightened by the vogue of the symposium—

at least, it is arithmetically intensified. An emblem of credence: four men and a moderator on a stage, sitting behind
a long table, each with his own glass and pitcher of water.
(Men also drink more water on the stage than women do,
and the effect of these pauses, unless the water spills, is again
sober and deliberate.) Even to an audience of faint impres-
sionability, it seems inconceivable that wisdom should not
issue from such an assemblage.

Women's voices also diminish their plausibility. Only
Mrs. Pankhurst ("Trust in God: She will provide") could
imagine a woman's voice coming out of a cumulus cloud or
a rhododendron bush. The blasphemer or idolator, hearing
it, would merely wince. During the first conversation on
earth Eve's voice caused Adam the first earache on earth.
In subsequent history this pain has persisted, impervious to
all efforts to control or eliminate its source. By Talmudic law
a man could divorce a wife whose voice could be heard next
door. From there to Shakespeare:

> *Her voice was ever soft,*
> *Gentle, and low—an excellent thing in woman.*

And to Yeats:

> *The women that I picked spoke sweet and low*
> *And yet gave tongue.*
> ("Hound Voice")

And to Samuel Beckett, guessing at the last torture, The
Worst: "a woman's voice perhaps, I hadn't thought of that,

they might engage a soprano." * The knowledge of this sound has permeated the intellectual conception of women, even of those who do not make public speeches. In the criticism of women's writing, not even the word *hysterical* recurs as regularly as *shrill.* The working rule: blame something written by a woman as *shrill,* praise something as *not shrill.*†

So the impression of a profound (or basso) authority is a property of men. But as a natural gift, like a waterfall, its regularity is its weakness: there is little to prevent its degenerating into no more than the means of identification. *That* is Niagara Falls, *this* is written by a man. Still, the *sensation* of authority remains, I think, the only test, like though less precise than that of litmus paper, by which one can distinguish between male and female prose. It is not that the written statement need have sexual content. For example, Lionel Abel has described his ideal theater critic:

> I want a man to go, first of all, not a woman (I do have some prejudices), and I want the man to be stoutly uneffeminate (still more prejudice). I do not want my critic to be an esthete.‡

* Samuel Beckett, *The Unnamable,* in *Molloy, Malone Dies* and *The Unnamable,* p. 505.

† At the most, women can hope for pity of the defect. Louis Auchincloss: "It is difficult [for women novelists] to avoid the strident note, the shrill cry; it is hard to keep from becoming a crank." (*Pioneers and Caretakers,* Minneapolis, University of Minnesota Press, 1965, p. 4.) For other *shrill*'s (or *shrillness*), see pp. 52, 78 and 130 of the same book.

‡ Lionel Abel, "Critique on a Critic," *Book Week,* September 18, 1966, p. 8.

A bulky phrase, *stoutly uneffeminate*, and yet this is not an instance of the idiom I have in mind. The *content* is of course thoroughly male—reproducing on the level of the theater the common American male aversion to women doctors or drivers—but the wording is not characteristic. The coy parenthetical admissions of irrationality are, on the contrary, just what one would suppose to be thinly effeminate.

At the same time, wordings central to this idiom may also be devoid of sexual opinion:

(1)

A generalization is in order at this point. Perhaps a third of future humanity will at some time during the course of their lives need an organ transplant. Terminal patients, victims of fatal accidents, condemned criminals who might be persuaded to will their healthy organs to society, and suicides, who number 22,000 a year in the United States, all die anyway. It will be a tragic waste if their organs are not made available to patients whose lives could be prolonged. With certain obvious qualifications, obtaining these organs involves questions of legal and social machinery rather than basic morality. We have not yet run quite full tilt into the moral dilemma.*

(2)

I know nothing of the circumstances surrounding Herbert Blau's resignation from the Lincoln Center Repertory Com-

---

* Roy L. Walford, M.D., "A Matter of Life and Death," *Atlantic*, August 1967, p. 70.

pany, but it is a melancholy decision for which we all bear some measure of responsibility. Blau's tenure with the company was far from distinguished; it is hard to think of a single play produced by him at the Vivian Beaumont that stimulated any real excitement, expectation, or sense of adventure. But given the quality of the man himself and of his past work, we must surely look to other causes than artistic inadequacy for some clue to his failure.*

(3)

Whether the "newer kind of shorter fiction"—be it a stylized snapshot as in Robbe-Grillet's "The Secret Room" or a "near-novel" as in Flannery O'Connor's "Wise Blood"—marks a genuine departure is a moot point. The stories gathered by Mr. Marcus may represent a rear-guard action, an after-life of the novel and the long tales of Conrad or Henry James. It is too early to tell. My own hunch is that the future of imaginative form lies elsewhere, in works part philosophic, part poetic, part autobiographical. It is, I think, the writings of Blake, of Nietzsche, of such solitary masters as Elias Canetti and Ernst Bloch, that contain the seeds of the next major literary genre. If the act of fiction is to reassert its claims on the adult mind, it will have to embody more knowledge, more intensity of thought and an awareness of language more in tune with that of Wittgenstein and Lévi-Strauss. What is, just now, more old-fashioned than a novel? †

* Robert Brustein, "Saturn Eats His Children," *New Republic*, January 28, 1967, p. 34.
† George Steiner, "The Search for New Genres," *Book Week*, December 11, 1966, p. 16.

The first statement sets off with an exemplary firmness, which opens the door for a bold prediction in turn. This prediction hurries past its own *perhaps* to appal the reader: must *a third* of all his descendants undergo this surgery? But to frighten is a subordinate effect of authority. Its chief effect is rather one of confidence, reason, adjustment and efficacy. These appear in the third sentence and come to an incomparable climax in the words *all die anyway*. How calmly the dead are found dead here! But no, there is regret—men may hang themselves anyway, but to bury their kidneys with them is a "tragic waste." In fact, the statement alienates the reader from the (defensible) goal of organ transplantation: why go to such lengths to keep bodies alive in a society habituated to accident, crime, capital punishment and despair?

But this is admittedly an extreme instance of the idiom. The topic, surgery, is in itself extreme. Only an exceptional self-confidence and aggressive purpose enable the surgeon to invade the body, which has for civilized laymen (except in moments of rage or hatred) a profound sanctity. One has to think of surgery as a virtuous barbarity, and expect barbaric terms to intrude upon explanations of its legitimate point of view. The second and third statements are more representative, however, in that they apply themselves to matters of no practical or physical urgency, and yet advance themselves along the same rhetorical route of authority as does the first statement. What unites the second and third is again the sensation of firmness, directness, confidence. They seem to me fair examples of critical prose now in this country, of an established masculine mode of speaking competently on esthetic issues. Particularly in the second passage, the decision with which even dull phrases are delivered makes them work. This decision dwindles somewhat in the third (where the *moot point* and the *hunch* are drains upon it), but here too the certainty with which even a predictable point is made establishes the effect of validity. "What is, just now, more old-fashioned than a novel?" For a moment, while he bears the weight of this question, the reader is subdued, and cannot at once remember that in fact nothing is, just now, more old-fashioned than the question itself.

It is possible, as well, that prolonged possession of real (as of illusive) authority, merely the habit of pronouncement, may carry this idiom, which is tolerable, to the verge of the insufferable. This is perhaps the covert occupational danger of any regular expression of opinions in public. Among our presidents, Johnson's terror of diffidence (which he equates with subtlety) is the rule, Lincoln's mildness is the exception. And at his best, Freud persuaded softly—he was too brilliant to assert. In the lecture on "Femininity," for example, his approach was elaborately tentative:

> If you reject this idea as fantastic and regard my belief in the influence of lack of a penis on the configuration of femininity as an *idée fixe*, I am of course defenceless.*

A ruse, a modest and disarming way of insuring one's safe conduct through dangerous and hostile territories.

* Sigmund Freud, "New Introductory Lectures on Psycho-Analysis," *Complete Psychological Works*, Vol. XXII, p. 132.

But of course I do not mean to suggest that the seemingly authoritative must be the obtuse as well. The following remarks on *Macbeth* are surely too unintelligible to be unintelligent:

> Manifestly, and, if not forthwith, certainly upon a moment's consideration, by all the motives prompting or circumstances attending the murder of Duncan that have been omitted, the big, sharply outlined, highly emotional contrast in the situation of a good man doing the deed of horror would be broken or obscured. If Macbeth had been thwarted or (to use Holinshed's word) "defrauded," as having, at this juncture, a better title to the throne than Malcolm, or had thought himself better fitted to rule; or, again, if Duncan had not borne his faculties so meek or been so clear in his great office, as in the tragedy but not the chronicle he is; why, then, Macbeth's conduct in killing him would have been more reasonable and more psychologically in keeping, to be sure, but less terrible, less truly tragic.*

The opening sentence is a physical experience, like a fishbone in the esophagus: it will not go up or down, there is agonized gulping, then the relief (after *consideration*) of a brief vomit of words. It is an expression of authority through caution, which is signalled by all those pussyfooting commas. Yielding, the reader thinks that what is finally said (what *is* finally said?) after so much hesitation must be the indubitable thing to say. And again:

* E. E. Stoll, "Source and Motive in Macbeth and Othello," in *From Shakespeare to Joyce* (New York, Doubleday, 1944), pp. 298–99.

The point is not at all to love one's brethren as oneself, since that is in defiance of all the laws of Nature, and since hers is the sole voice which must direct all the actions in our life; it is only a question of loving others as brothers, as friends given us by Nature, and with whom we should be able to live much better in a republican State, wherein the disappearances of differences must necessarily tighten the bonds.

The rational authority of the passage seems palpable: that businesslike *The point is*, the intimidating *laws of Nature*, the sweeping *sole voice* of moral guidance. Wordsworth comes to mind, and all our loose, benevolent and deadly dull associations with Nature. Rather than exhume them, we are prepared to submit at once to the new passage. By all means. To be sure. But this is the Marquis de Sade,* the closer bonds between men which interest him are seldom so canonized, and the denial of absolute love becomes, within a few paragraphs, the acceptance of murder.

Sade too, then, is an ambivalent instance. While his tone is that of rational authority, it is at the same time a wild distortion of that authority. His prose is built upon the incongruity of discursion and debauch, epitomized in the title "Philosophy in the Bedroom." So it becomes ultimately brash rather than judicious, and personal rather than public. It is the nineteenth century, rather than the eighteenth, with which one associates particularly the authoritative voice in writing —the voice which excludes the personal, the erratic or the insecure. Then, more than at any other time, confidence in the

* "Philosophy in the Bedroom," in *The Marquis de Sade* (New York, Grove Press, 1965), p. 309.

rational ordering of ideas seemed the primary motivation of prose. One might rename the eighteenth century, in liquid terms, the Age of the Teardrop, and let the nineteenth century become the Age of Saliva. In the first, the small perfect shape is as relevant as the *proof* or *evidence* of grief (or laughter). In the second exudation all is functional: the words are a continuous, indiscriminate and useful aid to the mastication of ideas. For all its occasional air of distress, the nineteenth century seems to have enjoyed the heartening belief that if calm minds set down their ordered, sequential and discreet thoughts, intellectual progress would certainly be made.

Once we are out of school, the eighteenth century seems to us far less determined to govern the abstract by means of immutable definitions, distinctions, generalizations—fixities. One might say that Jane Austen's contrast of sense and sensibility is just such a distinction. But then it is so small that it could never swell into the grand and public proportions of, say, Matthew Arnold's Hebraism and Hellenism. Similarly, much of English criticism in the eighteenth century avoids heaviness by being in verse, a form which does not recognize the separation of authority and delight. Pope's *Essay on Criticism* seems always tempted by, though it resists, the mockery of reason by rhyme*—by the pleasure of what W. H. Auden calls the "game" of poetry. Again, in Dr.

* Comparatively easy relations between the sexes, at least on the verbal level, are suggested, too, by Pope's readiness to appropriate phrases (such as "aromatic pain") from a woman poet—Anne, Countess of Winchelsea.

Johnson's criticism of Shakespeare, the most natural and innocent (we would say now *naive* or *subjective* or *effeminate*) statements of personal reaction—such as fear of the witches in *Macbeth*—are easily interspersed among acute and resounding judgments. Just as in the century before, for that matter, no fixed distinction can be kept between intellectual authority and intimate emotion in Donne's sermons.

But such a distinction is endemic to the nineteenth century. It was then, when women first began to publish not only as novelists but as (what we call) intellectuals, that a method of male utterance codified itself; and, as a result, a genuine difference seemed discernible between the ways in which men think and write, and the ways in which women think and write. They might publish simultaneously without risk of being confused. (Why, in turn, this confusion should be dreaded is complex, though certainly connected with the living, as opposed to the literary, dread that each sex experiences of being taken for the other.) So Dickens recorded his conviction that George Eliot's *Scenes from Clerical Life*, published anonymously, must be written by a woman. The dichotomy was established: the dominant and masculine mode possessing the properties of reason and knowledge, the subsidiary and feminine mode possessing feelings and intuitions. If this dichotomy was unreal, it was not less dedicated on the part, particularly, of the dominant mode. Until Oscar Wilde, a direct and progressive control of circumstances, however stubborn or ambiguous, seemed possible and desirable to all writers. Wilde disrupted a voluntary assumption of authority which had previously fit an involuntary sense of cultural condition.

One has the impression that the subsidiary mode was genuine, too—that, at any rate, as women still take part-time jobs more than men, women critics in the nineteenth century were gratified to discuss at least the feelings. It is impossible to believe that Mrs. Anna Jameson's comparison of Juliet and Thekla ("the German Juliet," the heroine of Schiller's *Wallenstein*) was disingenuous:

> The same confidence, innocence, and fervor of affection distinguish both heroines: but the love of Juliet is more vehement, the love of Thekla is more calm, and reposes more on itself; the love of Juliet gives us the idea of infinitude, and that of Thekla of eternity; the love of Juliet flows on with an increasing tide, like the river pouring to the ocean, and the love of Thekla stands unalterable, and enduring as the rock. In the heart of Thekla love shelters as in a home; but in the heart of Juliet he reigns a crowned king—"he rides on its pants triumphant!" *

I know, I know, both young women should be shut up for a year, with Mrs. Jameson, inside a computer. But still, Mrs. Jameson *thought out* that infinitude/eternity distinction, even though, exhausted by it, she collapses at once into the river/rock distinction.† I am rather fond of Mrs. Jameson:

* Mrs. Anna Jameson, *Shakespeare's Heroines*, 1832 (New York, A. L. Burt, undated), p. 77.

† Water, as Freud would observe, is often Mrs. Jameson's undoing: "There is in the beauty of Cordelia's character an effect too sacred for words, and almost *too deep for tears*, within her heart is a *fathomless*

her bad is worse, but her worst is incomparable, as here in her acrobatic pleasure in the notion of heartbeat-riding.

Also, it would be dishonest not to admit that Mrs. Jameson is still alive. To admit as well that in her present senility she seems to have lost both her old occasional pertinence and her constant integrity. Now not only what are called "ladies' novels" (*The Valley of the Dolls, The Shadow Wife,* etc.), but more reputable observations of writers like Anaïs Nin or Rebecca West repeat the ritual gestures of sensibility, just as some men repeat those of authority. The one seems essentially no more anachronistic than the other, but these women strain what was from the start a subsidiary mode, whereas these men merely prolong the dominant mode of a century. Though the one is as dubious as the other, we too continue involuntarily to anticipate cerebral benefits and emotional injuries.

This is perhaps why we daily anticipate the worst of our own time, since the authoritative mode is no longer the mode of original, which is more than competent, expression. At the same time, the exertion of sensibility is not marked in the most interesting writing by women now. So the very distinction I have tried to characterize will not apply consistently to either the men or the women whom we now admire most. Extremes, of course, of anachronism are still easily categorized. I should guess that a particular aridity, what seems a

---

well of purest affection, but its *waters sleep* in silence and obscurity,—never failing in their *depth* and never *overflowing* in their fullness." [My italics.] (*Shakespeare's Heroines,* p. 228.)

160

systematic dehydration of a subject, is still for us not only obviously academic but obviously male:

> The fourth set of images is provided through Dilsey's reflecting angle of vision. Implicitly and symbolically there is an analogous relationship between Dilsey's emphasis on certain basic, primary, positive values throughout and Ben's intuitive sense of values. Thus, the positive angles of vision, mirrored by Ben and Dilsey most sharply in the first and fourth structural parts of *The Sound and the Fury*, may be considered literally and symbolically as bracketing and containing the two negative angles of vision mirrored by Quentin and Jason in the second and third parts. Taken in this sense, the structural arrangement of these four hinged mirrors serves to heighten the reader's awareness of Faulkner's major thematic antithesis between the chaos-producing effects of self-love and the order-producing effects of compassionate and self-sacrificial love in human experience.*

This plane lands at Laputa in fifteen minutes. One might protest that this is simply graduate-school prose, as it is written by both men and women students. But it is the prose of nineteenth-century scholars (and men), particularly in Germany, which has in the past been set as the graduate-school model. In this way, it is true, some women may emerge as such writers; but this mode is for them even

* Lawrance Thompson, "Mirror Analogues in *The Sound and the Fury*," *The Modern American Novel*, ed. Max Westbrook (New York, Random House, 1966), p. 153.

more imitative than for men, an intellectual transvestism as well as a cultural affectation.

Again, one might say that the mode of authority persists in Norman Mailer and is immediately identifiable as male:

> The fact of the matter is that the prime responsibiilty of a woman probably is to be on earth long enough to find the best mate possible for herself, and conceive children who will improve the species.*

The fact of the matter, the prime responsibility, the stock phrasing of the mode—and yet, the passage has an undercurrent of parody. It is provocative nonsense, Darwinian drivel, designed to ruffle rather than to instruct. Mailer's game, and I admire it, is to announce with the old air of authority what is erratic or capricious, to substitute indignities for dignity. He practices, what he would be bound to call, an *existential* whimsicality, a mockery of responsible thought which fits a time when the conventional responsibilities have fallen into rote. An air then of rational certitude can become the means of stating the totally inventive:

> If we eat a bland food, a food we can dominate completely, that is to say a food whose character, whose—permit me—whose echo of the soul, is compliant, tender, passive to our seizure of it, we satisfy something masculine in ourselves. A man with ulcers is burning with the masculine need to dominate details in his life he simply cannot dominate. So in drinking milk, a bland food, a food more feminine than himself, he can

* Norman Mailer, *The Presidential Papers*, p. 130.

discharge this backed-up masculinity. But of course he uses up masculinity in eating bland food, he alters his proportions.*

That is, Mailer manages one solution of our present impediment to prose, the incompatibility of authority and uncertainty, by an outrageous abuse of authoritative tone. To write anything, of course, even a note to the milkman, is to claim *some* authority. A sentence is an admission, reluctant or eager, of the writer's supposing others might benefit by knowing he has completed a thought. One must value the action in order to expose it, and assume that the sentence has not only a subject and a verb but its own mite of validity. But as people have not lived before in less valid or less comprehensible times, the full tone of authority seems prolix or monotonous or exhausted. We are deprived, by our situation in events, of our taste for the stentorian in statements: this deprivation is perhaps what is meant by references to the *womanization* of the times. If a whole age has cut itself, it does not welcome lectures on glass blowing. There is a sense now in which it welcomes only the writing which deliberately relinquishes the tone of authority or, like Mailer's, abuses it. Both are devices of continuing to speak at all.

Writing now involves a subterranean embarrassment, which we commonly associate with feminine rather than masculine statement; and this embarrassment issues in the cultivation, on the part of the talented, of either modesty or rashness—again both, in the past, conventional aspects of femininity. Even before, as in the quotation from Freud,

* Norman Mailer, *Cannibals and Christians*, p. 293.

163

some discursive writing established a kind of androgynous zone in which authority was not exaggerated, in which confidence was mitigated by abashment. Varieties of the disruption of authority have now, however, proliferated as they have become essential, rather than simply preferred, as the means of speaking to one's own time:

> Life is a little like disease, with its crises and periods of quiescence, its daily improvements and setbacks. But unlike other diseases life is always mortal. It admits of no cure. It would be like trying to stop up the holes in our body, thinking them to be wounds. We should die of suffocation almost before we were cured.*

One would not immediately associate this remark of Italo Svevo's with one of Norman Mailer's. *Life is a little like disease* is quieter than Mailer. What connects the two is the grotesque turn of thought, the expression (ostensibly rational) of an eccentric perception. To think of the orifices of the body as wounds, the mind has to have wriggled through a tunnel of established conceptions to emerge at once chastened and bold, able to see things as they might look to an anarchic eye, an eye never governed by incarnation.

In a sense, then, both Svevo and Mailer elude the old authority, though the one affects timidity and the other courage in doing so. Other vogues of disruption of the rational are perhaps more sensational at the moment, and more

---

* Italo Svevo, *The Confessions of Zeno*, pp. 410–11.

patently recreative of what were previously considered feminine habits of thought; though they are also, I think, less subtle than the irrationality of Svevo. There is the preference of Marshall McLuhan, for example, for the hypothetical, impulsive, frankly improbable "probe," or that of Norman O. Brown for the inspired and sibylline:

> There is eternal recurrence; there are "eternal objects" (Whitehead); archetypes. This is a hard lesson. There is a sense in which war cannot be abolished (*Love's Body*, p. 182). Or, there is an eternal object of which war is a false image, or inadequate idea. The thing to be abolished is literalism; the worship of false images; idolatry. Allen Ginsberg saw it just the way it is: Moloch. A false idol fed with real victims. This is no joke. (Nor is fire; Heraclitean fire.) *

In comparison to Brown, Mrs. Jameson takes on a frigid, algebraic aspect which is quite odd for her. And yet one knows this new statement is written by a man. The Heraclitean fire is smoky, wisps of the old stances come swirling up. The grim paternal warnings: *This is a hard lesson. This is no joke.* The vested commas and semicolons. And that irresistible solipsism (shared with Matthew Arnold!) of referring students to the authority of one's own previous publications. Half Pan, half G. L. Kittredge.

Unexpectedly, as though one found that some frivolous expenditure was practical after all, in this new idiom women writers move about with an ease they could not feel

* Norman O. Brown, "A Reply to Herbert Marcuse," *Commentary*, March 1967, p. 83.

before. Again, I am not speaking of those who relentlessly prolong our evening with Elizabeth Barrett Browning (they will *not* get up and say, "Enough of this lucrative distress. Call me a cab."). Instead, I hope to define the way in which it is now possible for women to write well. Quite simply, having not had physical or intellectual authority before, they have no reason to resist a literature at odds with authority. There are, of course, those who prefer instead to wear hand-me-downs, to borrow now the certitude of the nineteenth century. One might say that the defect of Simone de Beauvoir is the authority of her prose: the absence of hesitation in hesitant times amounts to a presence, a tangible deficiency, a sense of obtuseness.

In better work by women now, while sentiment is avoided as stigmatic (as the inimical mark of their sex in others' minds), authority too is skirted—again, as in Mailer and Svevo, by deliberate rashness or by ironic constraint. The tenor of Mary McCarthy's remarks on *Macbeth* is rather different from that of E. E. Stoll's:

> He is a general and has just won a battle; he enters the scene making a remark about the weather. "So fair and foul a day I have not seen." On this flat note Macbeth's character tone is set. "Terrible weather we're having." "The sun can't seem to make up its mind." "Is it hot/cold/wet enough for you?" A commonplace man who talks in commonplaces, a golfer, one might guess, on the Scottish fairways, Macbeth is the only Shakespeare hero who corresponds to a bourgeois type: a murderous Babbitt, let us say.

166

> Macbeth has absolutely no feeling for others except envy, a
> common middle-class trait. He *envies* the murdered Duncan
> his rest, which is a strange way of looking at your victim.*

At once a comical and a suicidal wit: the intention of wit
exceeds that of justice or plausibility. What is said is said
more naturally and more quickly than what Stoll says, and
the opinion of Macbeth is engaging. But wrong. One doesn't
for a minute *accept* Macbeth as the general, the golfer, the
Eisenhower. And the Babbitt reference is quite dead, like a
hemline of the late thirties. The point of view is feminine,
in the pejorative sense, not only in its wifely depreciation of
Macbeth (Lady Macbeth's "good sense" is later preferred
to Macbeth's "simple panic"), but also in its social narrowness. In its determination to make Macbeth middle-class, the
criticism is middle-class itself. It is hard to imagine a more
philistine conception of envy than that "common middle-
class trait." But it is the rashness of the judgment which re-
deems it, its daring, its mocking diminution of a subject
which God knows had taken on an institutionalized gran-
deur.† The rashness links Mary McCarthy, for all their

---

* Mary McCarthy, "General Macbeth," *Harper's*, June 1962, pp. 35
and 37.

† It is perhaps necessary to distinguish between varieties of rashness.
The rashness of Mary McCarthy, which ousts conventional attitudes,
is not the rashness, say, of Rebecca West: "We were not alone. The
house was packed with little girls, aged from twelve to sixteen, in the
care of two or three nuns. They were, like any gathering of their kind
in any part of the world, more comfortable to look at than an English
girls' school. They were apparently waiting quite calmly to grow up.

disagreements, with Norman Mailer; the diminution with Svevo, and with now.

The wit there is arrogant, as it is not in this comment of Colette's upon literary prodigies:

> I admire child gymnasts, but I am a little afraid of child writers. To start with, there are too many of them. Then who in the world would not be afraid of a child's vigour and ease of movement through the impenetrable? He lacks only our vocabulary to be our equal when the passion to write comes upon him. I could give the name, at any rate the pseudonym she has chosen to write under, of more than one girl of fifteen whose literary baggage already comprises a slim volume of poems, two plays, three if not more novels, and *Memoirs* (sic). There is the same facility among boys. Of course I feel no pressing hurry to form an opinion on so many youthful works, confided to me as they are without my consent. But I still retain my faculty for astonishment, even if it should only be

---

They expected it, and so did the people looking after them. There was no panic on anybody's part. There were none of the unhappy results which follow the English attempt to make all children look insipid and docile, and show no signs whatsoever that they will ever develop into adults. There were no little girls with poked chins and straight hair, aggressively proud of being plain, nor were there pretty girls making a desperate precocious proclamation of their femininity. But, of course, in a country where there is very little homosexuality, it is easy for girls to grow up into womanhood." (*Black Lamb and Grey Falcon*, Vol. I, p. 163.)

The final generalization is the clue: a person is obviously rash to allow herself to say anything so simple-silly. But the rashness is placid and auntlike. In the end, it reiterates an old point of view rather than risking a new one.

for youthful writers' attempts to exploit their own novelty. Sometimes, it is true, they conceal their identity, but they never forget to state their age.*

A muted, light and precious animosity, in contrast to Mary McCarthy's. But the contradiction is superficial, in that all wit is the means of relinquishing authority, of deprecating the importance not only of the subject but of the writer as well. And it is this predisposition which moves men and women writers closer together now. The same impulses at once to diminish and to amuse occur in Elizabeth Hardwick's description of Boston:

> Harvard (across the river in Cambridge) and Boston are two ends of one moustache. Harvard is now so large and international it has altogether avoided the whimsical stagnation of Boston. But the two places need each other, as we knowingly say of a mismatched couple. . . .†

Behind such a passage lies the persuasion that prose, as Auden argues that poetry, can no longer be written in the public or loudspeaker voice. The persuasion too, that, within judgment and so within *some* assumption of authority, still there must be conscious reduction. Repeatedly, the large and the unknown are compressed into terms of the small and known.

The opposite tendency is to enlarge. Even the inhibited

* Colette, *The Blue Lantern*, translated by Roger Senhouse (New York, Farrar, Straus, 1963), pp. 93–94.
† Elizabeth Hardwick, "Boston," in *A View of My Own* (New York, Farrar, Straus, 1951), p. 154.

Stoll passage on Macbeth is in the end an enlargement: if one must be so cautious in saying a thing, then it must be a large and important thing to say. But enlargement too can be given a modern form. What was thought to be small and known, and therefore not meaningful, such as Mailer's glass of milk, is scrutinized again, and swells out into the bizarre "echo of the soul." There are heroic confrontations but they take place in the *small* intestine. And even as such topics of disquisition, carrots and eggs, disturb our sense of proper or authoritative enlargement, so the circumstances in which they are discussed seem deliberately to deride their official or public significance. Like Sade's "Philosophy in the Bedroom," Mailer's "Metaphysics of the Belly" is shielded against formality by disparateness.

I have perhaps not helped at all those obsessed readers like Dickens who are bent upon identifying the sex of writers. But I could not promise that the second distinction would be foolproof, and, except on its lower levels (those of popular sentiment for women and of reputable competence for men), it seems now less trustworthy than ever before. As both simple authority and simple sensibility have become anachronistic, writers cohabit an area of prose in which sudden alternations of the reckless and the sly, the wildly voluble and the laconic, define only a mutual and refreshing disturbance of mind.

I have confined the point of authoritative tone, by thinking of it almost exclusively in terms of critical prose.

Meanwhile, the present approaches to poetry and to fiction are quite similar to those which affect criticism as well. Auden, as I have said, remarks on the impossibility of the public voice, and chooses for himself the private, personal and casual. He will not seem to do more than the simplest person can do, i.e., speak to one other person. But as this choice is the poetic equivalent of critical modesty, so there are poets, like prose writers, who choose just as deliberately to be rash and immoderate. Allen Ginsberg and Andrei Vozneshensky coincide in the conviction that poetry must now be more than public—beyond secular authority, *prophetic*. Poets may choose now to play either penitent or priest, but no one wants to be prime minister.

Similarly in fiction, the often tedious discussion of "point of view" probably reflects, again, a backing away from authority. This is expressed in a dismissal of the "omniscient author." The preference has become popular (in fact, by now equally commonplace) for the narrator who is presumably like any reader: imperfectly informed, confused, insecure in judgment—a part of, rather than a commentator upon, the story. And if this fallibility is not felt (or affected), another withholding of authority occurs—in which an interpretative faculty is still not directly exercised. The total comprehension, on the part of the writer, of his created situation is merely implied by the factual terms in which he, seemingly by necessity and with the utmost economy, puts the situation forward.

Alternatively, these forms of reluctance to speak yield to the relaxation of the sentence into its least strenuous, least

171

emphatic and least periodic form. This relaxation is an equal denial of authority, but the first qualities put forward in its place are tentative: an acknowledgement of minute qualifications, a fidelity to all flickers and tremors of sensation. In this kind of sentence, especially, the sense of the manipulation of experience yields entirely to the sense of its sheer reception. Virginia Woolf was inclined to consider the new sentence as sexually characteristic, as a "woman's sentence":

> She [Dorothy Richardson] has invented, or, if she has not invented, developed and applied to her own uses, a sentence which we might call the psychological sentence of the feminine gender. It is of a more elastic fibre than the old, capable of stretching to the extreme, of suspending the frailest particles, of enveloping the vaguest shapes. Other writers of the opposite sex have used sentences of this description and stretched them to the extreme. But there is a difference. Miss Richardson has fashioned her sentence consciously, in order that it may descend to the depths and investigate the crannies of Miriam Henderson's consciousness. It is a woman's sentence, but only in the sense that it is used to describe a woman's mind by a writer who is neither proud nor afraid of anything that she may discover in the psychology of her sex.*

But, in fact, it seems impossible to determine a sexual sentence. As Virginia Woolf herself makes clear, the only certain femininity is in Dorothy Richardson's subject. Her sentence has more in common with Henry James's or Joyce's

* Virginia Woolf, *Contemporary Writers* (New York, Harcourt, Brace & World, 1966), pp. 124–25.

than with, say, George Eliot's. The description of a sound from *Pilgrimage:*

> The sound of reading came from the den—a word-mouthing, word-slurring monotonous drawl—thurrah, thurrah, thurrah; thurrah, thurrah . . . a single beat, on and on, the words looped and forced into it without any discrimination, the voice dropping uniformly at the end of each sentence . . . *thrab.* . . . An Early Victorian voice, giving reproachful instruction to a child . . . a class of board-school children reciting. . . . Perhaps they had changed their minds about going out. . . .*

The means by which such a consciousness expresses itself emerge from its inwardness rather than its femininity. The rhetorical shift is one from effect upon visible circumstances to that of registration of unseen impressions. The implication is again modest, in that judgment, or even comprehension, of the whole scene is not pretended. Nothing is asserted beyond the impression of the whole upon a single, living and (however sensitive) limited witness. The only remaining arrogance, though it alone can sometimes become palpable, is the conviction that the witness's impressions have significance.

At the same time, as in poetry, a contrary allegiance to extravagance is apparent in fiction, perhaps particularly in American fiction—a deliberate rhetorical swinging-out beyond previous bounds. This is the first and most striking

---

* Dorothy Richardson, "The Tunnel," *Pilgrimage* (New York, Alfred A. Knopf, 1967), Vol. II, p. 61.

aspect of William Gass's *Omensetter's Luck*, of Norman Mailer's *Why Are We in Vietnam?*, of John Barth's *The Sot-Weed Factor* and *Giles Goat-Boy*—where pleasure is taken in reproduction, in the mock-revival (appropriate to the fundamental shift from sobriety) of extinct tones of authority. It is clear in such work that the conventional ban on omniscience is a critical half-truth. Only the stolid and straightforward assumption of omniscience now seems insupportable, the unqualified assumption of understanding. The same quality which will no longer do in the game warden is instead sought out in the goat or the rhinoceros.

It must be said for the authoritative mode, however, that an appetite for it, as for any illusion of certitude, is still strong. This is met by a general capacity to write in the mode, as it is least difficult to write out of a common past and common training—in pronouncement, in definition, in exposition (the freshman theme: Describe a mechanical process. Analyze the character of a person whom you know *well*). It is perhaps for this reason that more people write and more read conventional critical writing now than before. They can't be assumed to *care* more for fact and opinion and theory than others have. Nonfiction, on the whole, is now simply the easiest and most familiar (and, at the same time, useful) ambiance of words which is left. An equivalent authority in the conventional novel has slipped beneath intelligence, been exiled now to our vast Siberian reaches of vulgarity. But intelligence in turn is a limited reading quality. It lags behind the difficulties of innovation and therefore clings now to the last reputable area of convention.

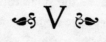

V

RESPONSES

there must have been a time
when things were looser
a time between gas and solid
when things could shift about
imagine seeing through people
or whatever we were then
and hugging vapor to vapor
or jelly to jelly
that was an inventive time

—Edward Field, "Jellyfish Invasion"
from *Stand Up, Friend, With Me.*

૭§ I am eager to describe the small capacity or inclination of many women for executive sexuality, that mode of sexual thinking which is primarily forceful, economical, forthright and decisive.

While they provide little evidence of a superior delicacy of feelings, women tend to be skeptical of what can be achieved by physical force. After all, they are certain of losing if they involve themselves. Their first comment on the football game or the prize fight, "It's so pointless," means, "It would be pointless for me to take part." With modern weapons, of course, and with the modern integration of combatants and noncombatants (children too are committed to war now in the sense that, like their parents, they are wounded and killed), this distinction of feebleness may diminish. Women are already soldiers in the North Vietnamese army and, behind the lines, in the Israeli army. Still, in our minds the distinction persists. Out of that cowardice to which all the weak are more subject than the strong, women continue to withdraw from violence. And in the United States, this withdrawal holds them apart from a major preoccupation of the society. The only available reconciliation is an emphasis, like Norman Mailer's, upon women's pleasure in seeing violence done.* But this suggests again the fallacy of balance and compensation: men do, women watch; the cast has an audience, the Scotch takes soda. In fact, men watch too. Everyone is available to that taste; and since it is vicarious, it still does not constitute full participation in the predominant mode.

Moreover, watchers vary in their reactions to spectacle. They may as easily grow confused or tired as dedicated. Women must be partially conscious, in witnessing any disorder (however apparently purposeful or deliberate), of emerging from disorder as well. Their physiology is not one from which confidence in executive procedure can be extracted. Menstruation proves that the body carries out expensive, time-consuming and futile operations. The retraction of the uterine wall, which leaves the inflated veins to atrophy, break open and lose their absurd provisions for a non-event, constitutes an image of repeated bankruptcy. A monthly reminder that failure is as likely as success, and that failure may sometimes be as welcome as success—principles which, obviously, do not govern our society.

Nothing else in human physiology, except perhaps aging, is comparable to the eerie abstraction of this process. Its resolute private timing seems mad. The sane purpose of

* The opinion is revived, rather than conceived, by Mailer. The Marquis de Sade: "Would you meet them [women]? Announce a cruel spectacle, a burning, a battle, a combat of gladiators, you will see droves of them come running; but these occasions are not numerous enough to feed their fury: they contain themselves, and they suffer." ("Philosophy in the Bedroom," *The Marquis de Sade*, p. 255.)

punctuality is an encounter between one thing and another—an editor and his desk, a farmer and his cow. Even aging meets at least death. But the menstrual schedule is precise, while the conception it anticipates occurs capriciously. It is like an alarm clock going off in an empty bedroom, or a mentally disturbed computer. There is even, about the schedule, an unnerving suggestion of its being all the more compulsively, for being pointlessly, timed. It observes only the Archimedean rule by which the intensity of physical forces mounts in inverse ratio to their rational purpose—as rain falls most heavily on picnics.

Nothing much in the vociferous opinions of others concerning the functions of women encourages them, either, in moral decision. It is impossible for women to consider themselves with the unqualified rapture or the unqualified horror through which they move. Inhabiting the only form there is for them to inhabit, they cannot find it simply heroic—the asylums, in that case, would swarm with victims of a Ceres complex. Nor is it possible for women to accept the opposite judgment of their own loathsomeness, and continue to live. So they find it hard to honor the wife and dishonor the prostitute, to dispense these moral merits and demerits with the standard celerity. The prostitute in what was, until recently, called Women's Court: a Daumier sketch, female in center of males, a creature not calculated to enhance, for other creatures like her, the effect of consistency in our sexual ethic. On the contrary, not taking part in the prostitute's employment or her punishment, other women tend (obtusely) to confuse the two as superficial, night-and-day variations

of *use*. Next to the pleasure of reading pornography is
of deciding whether or not such reading should be for\
den. So we inexorably arrive at public essays, such as George
Steiner's "Night Words," on the importance of erotic privacy. To become so doubly engaged, one must have not only
appetite, but the illusion of one's authority to direct the
appetite of others. But women, like many Negroes, may cease
to endorse either the elevation or denigration of themselves,
and so reject the prevailing habit of extreme differentiation.
Christ honored only the mother who conceived without intercourse and the prostitute who resigned from it. So they
were alike, after all, and both at fault in the sexual form
which God the Father had presumably designed for them.

It is difficult to endorse such absolute judgments when the
sense of sexual experience is relative. The insistence of one
form upon contrasting itself with the other suggests that
there may be only contrast.* Its validity fades before its
evident compulsion. One is left with an odd impression of
contrast as the only means of continuance, as though life

---

* Even the physical vanity of women seems more comparative than that
of men. Essential nature is less fixed for them: they hold themselves constantly under reconsideration in the light of other women: "They had
not permitted themselves to feel resentment because they knew from the
phone operator that there was a girl in the picture, and they had, one
and all, persuaded themselves that she must be infinitely more beautiful
and glamorous than they were. In this way, their own charms were not
called into question. If a man prefers, say, Greta Garbo to you, it does
not mean that you are not perfectly all right in your own style, not perfectly adequate to any of the usual requirements." (Mary McCarthy,
"Portrait of the Intellectual as a Yale Man," from *The Company She
Keeps*.)

were defined as the lungs' compulsion to contrast the properties of oxygen and carbon dioxide. Or as Genet describes the imposed monosexuality of the men's prison, in which some men must become pseudowomen in order that all the customary sexual, psychological and social distinctions may persist, artificially. The habit of each sex is to define the inadequacies of the other, and then to love or hate them. Whichever has the larger opportunity to speak defines the more loudly. At all intellectual levels. In a single issue of *Life* Magazine, there have been (1) the White House chef claiming that no woman can make grasshopper pie as good as his, and (2) the poet John Berryman shouting, All women poets are spinsters or Lesbians! But why does he care? What is the implied interdependence of good poetry and heterosexual experience? Does Mr. Berryman suppose the imprimatur of his own work is his own copulative history? But, of course, the most immediate means of aggrandizing whatever one does is to say that no one of the opposite sex could do it. Each cries out for its own matchlessness. And it is this cry, that She cannot do as well as He, which batters the more ears—and which therefore, inevitably, discourages the commitment of women to our social professions.

It is equally difficult, physiologically, for women to aspire to the sexual virtues of purpose, foresight and economy. The pre-eminent shrewdness, for example, with which Henry Miller's protagonist, in *The Tropic of Cancer* (and *in flagrante*), steals his bus fare home from his partner's abandoned purse. A woman might do the same, but I think with less sense of her election thereby to Everywoman. Pleasure

or profit seems more easily interpreted as Duty or Destiny
by men. Keeping the commandment to "increase and multiply" coincides more neatly for them with natural inclination.

At the same time, women cannot help observing that conception (their highest virtue, by all reports) simply happens
or doesn't. It lacks the style of enterprise. It can be prevented
by foresight and device (though success here, as abortion
rates show, is exaggerated), but it is accomplished by luck
(good or bad). Purpose often seems, if anything, a deterrent.
A devious business benefiting by indirection, by pretending
not to care, as though the self must trick the body. In the
regrettable conception, the body instead tricks the self—
much as it does in illness or death. It is probably in consequence of this physical sense of double-dealing that women
do not—at any rate, convincingly—endorse evangelical
views of sexual intercourse. Sober self-congratulation is impeded for them by the ever-present possibility of becoming
the butt of a joke.

Nor can women think properly in terms of the conserva-
tion or frugal distribution of sexual materials.* The easy
fusion, for men, of a capitalistic and physical ethic must be-
muse women, whose chief sexual (if not spiritual) charac-

---

* At the present time, thrift is repeatedly urged in every interchange
between the self and what is not the self. If materials must be lost to the
outer world, the loss must be regretted, or at least *studied*. In *About the
House*, Auden expresses gratification in the achievement of normal and
regular bowel movements, and Norman Mailer "reads" feces like tea
leaves—modern "sermons in stones." From this point of view, it is interesting that Malamud should assign Jakov Bok (in *The Fixer*) the job
of supervising truckloads of bricks.

teristic is an ungovernable extravagance. In fact, to any entrepreneur except nature, the human female would seem too wasteful an item to be kept in stock.

This extravagance is even external. The breasts are largely gratuitous to any economy of sex. During their adult lives, women carry this excess baggage everywhere—and almost always aimlessly, like two empty picnic hampers. Yet in the past, when Western upper-class pregnancies were more numerous and when no convenient substitute for breast milk was available (i.e., when breasts were most economical), nursing was instead considered socially degrading. According to their caste, women provided milk for all infants, much as cows do now, or for none at all. An infant, like the first child of the Sigmund Freuds, might scream with hunger while its mother and father waited for the wet nurse to arrive. (The Freuds waited for two wet nurses in turn. The first, according to Freud, did nothing but eat *his* food.) And now, when nursing has become optional, a practice one chooses or declines according to temperament, the breasts take on a macabre physiological (if not erotic) character. How they engorge themselves, swelling into great red throbbing tumors of pain, when the woman "decides" not to nurse the child. In comparison, Van Itallie's making them of plasticine (in his play *Motel*) is an innocuous grotesquerie. At the same time, the use of the breasts having declined as their susceptibility to cancer remains stable (or rather increases, as a correlation between breast-feeding and resistance to cancer is generally assumed), they indicate death more than life. Like out-of-season fruits, they exemplify two forms of marketing waste—display and decay.

But then, all productions of the female body are slow and burdensome: the dropsical heaviness which can precede menstruation, the monstrous weight of pregnancy. Menopausal disturbances are relieved by combined diuretics and tranquillizers—to drain off excesses of both water and emotion. So much for the spiritual significance of either. (Or does the body, in this way, offer intimations of some immortal dismay?) And the release of all these materials is Tolstoyan, reckless: the body is freed rather than deprived of its property. One might take as characteristic the indifference of women, after childbirth, to the disposition of their placentae. An indifference corrected by those models of our economy, the drug manufacturers, who put the placentae to (their second) profitable use by extracting hormones from them. The Victorian correlation between sexual discharges and money,* and the consequent recommendations of sexual budgeting, persist in masculine and provident, rather than in feminine and improvident, contexts.

This variation in attitude attaches particularly to pregnancy. To speak of this condition as one of gain or increment (something in the oven, etc.) is a simplification natural to the observer (axiom: what grows larger must be richer) and impossible for the participant. No intellectual or emotional commitment to pregnancy can erase the physical

* This correlation is discussed by Steven Marcus in his *The Other Victorians.*

sense, if not of invasion, at least of inconvenience. Colette recalls having looked "like a rat with a stolen egg": the acquisition may be precious but it is also extremely awkward. It always seems desirable, at the proper time, to put it down someplace. Delivery is as much a relief as an achievement. Literally, one gets rid of a foreign body. (In *My Secret Life*, a pregnant country girl is called "poisoned.") And this relief seems to have no moral relevance, it indicates no connubial or maternal vice or virtue. It is only an intense variety of the individual and amoral pleasure of any convalescence, in which the person newly appreciates mere existence. Conventional sexual economics are too simple, since the pleasure in the child is complexly one of both profit *and* loss.

So women come to seem deciduous, men evergreen. Things fall from women, repeatedly, cyclically. With marriage, they drop even their last names (unless they're English girls, in which case they sometimes hyphenate their names with their husbands'. The éclat of this punctuation justifies the hint of sexual parity). Ordinarily, even couples named Beasley want boys, else the-name-will-die-out. Girls lose their virginity too, more markedly than boys (in Algeria, the bloodied sheet is still exhibited to the wedding guests)—or their reputation, or both. Next they lose babies in miscarriage; or, allowed the natural posture of childbirth, they drop them at full term. Eventually they lose the capacity itself for experiencing these former losses. Even the uterus, the pear standing on its stem, tends to fall over, as though wearying of its inane poise. At the same time, the chins, the breasts and the belly sag. The flesh of the arms hangs from the bones, like a wet wash on the line.

Of course, women are not quite alone in this losing. At the end of *Finnegans Wake*, Anna Livia Plurabelle is tired of humanity (or all men) and "all the lazy leaks down over their brash bodies." But more often, in societies which have plumped for gaining only, even young women suggest its twin losing too keenly. Though the young of both sexes feed upon fantasies of the power of their bodies over others, these fantasies are diluted for girls by a concomitant fear of the effect of their bodies upon themselves. The possibility of pregnancy still constitutes an innate insecurity. Dreams of domination are disturbed by the chance of being so dominated. The charm of young girls' irresponsibility, of their tyrannical caprices, is that everyone knows, in fact, they are fish flirting with the net—bound to be caught, and soon, in consequence. (Donne: "For thou thyself art thine own bait.") It is perhaps in stubborn reaction that the emphasis upon their giving birth, upon their ability and readiness to introduce new lives, is blatant. The most remarkable human voiding may then, in turn, be thought of as fulfillment, and the implication of the parents' end be obscured in the child's beginning. Their joy, too, modifies this implication. It is clearer in that mixture of pleasure and comic distress with which people become grandparents.

The sexual responsibility of women is inevitable, proper. But nature, in this matter, seems excessively subsidized by society. It is as though the female body, more subtly fascistic in its intents than the male, was nonetheless felt to be

185

an insufficient obstacle to license or insouciance. The society must lend its help, to island the bodies in vast seas of words about them. An inescapable attention is repeatedly cautioned against inattention—nothing is more lucrative, I suppose, than manuals of popular gynecology. The advertisements, for example, of Dr. Eric Trimmer's *Femina* sang the invariable duet of purposes: (1) the renovation of the libido and (2) the detection of disease. These are only superficially incompatible—like frequenting and sentencing prostitutes, sweating and freezing, part of the diurnal advance and retreat. One is to be enticed by sample revelations of *Femina*:

> Can a missed period be a symptom of a disease completely unrelated to the reproductive tract?

> What symptom may suggest the need for increasing the frequency of intercourse?*

A blind passion for the gas-meter man, no doubt, or biting the dog's ear. Underlying all these joys of speculation, however, the play is upon two sources of anxiety: (1) the uniform suspicion that some female bodies are doing tricks that other female bodies haven't learned, and (2) the uniform suspicion that all female bodies take nasty advantage of the least diversion of interest from themselves. The reading prospect for men is one of morbid titillation, for women one of relentless self-scrutiny. The society's twin deities of sensation and hygiene exact the tribute of feminine narcissism.

* *New York Times Book Review*, November 6, 1966, p. 49.

This commentary upon themselves may be easy for women to disbelieve, but it carries the obligation of notice. It becomes hard, then, to estimate the degree of feminine dissociation which results merely from tedium. Women live like subjects of a bureaucracy in which they must read interminable and triplicated forms, whether or not they agree to sign them in the end. Their self-consciousness grows with their reading, so that educated women tend, by twenty-seven, to walk about like sensate editorials on the Woman Problem. They are not allowed to escape the sense of species, they are like giraffes reading Lamarck every morning before they stretch their necks. At the least, then, boredom widens the gap between directive and inclination, between public dogma and individual, though often silent, heresy. Deceptive acquiescence has been prolonged through centuries—the only guile by which the unconvinced get along in the midst of irascible conviction. The present American moment, when incredulity amounts to a national trait, perhaps accommodates women best, wryly enough: a dubious condition has always been more familiar to the one sex than to the other.

For the woman writer, the simplest trimming of the sails has been to pretend more than endorsement of prevailing opinions: *enthusiasm* for them. A naked person in a society converted to clothing can at least write odes in praise of overcoats. But even this guile is variable. One feels it to be unconscious in some writers, who deceive themselves along with their audience (as parents fall asleep reading bedtime stories aloud)—entirely calculated in others, and then in others of both sexes.* Moreover, it is often hard to know where conviction ends and calculation begins. And calculation may be too hard a word; in some writers, it seems rather a self-deceptive vanity. It is possible for the vain to associate themselves with the best that has been said, and to associate *other* women with the worst: to court the authorities, like state's witnesses, by admitting the guilt of their associates. When Anaïs Nin writes, "Man attacks the vital center. Woman fills out the circumference," and then, "Feminine vision is usually myopic. I do not think mine is . . ." † we know that she herself does not intend to subsist circumferentially.

But it is apparent too that, while men and women employ the same feminine stereotypes, the woman writer seems the more offensive in doing so:

> Man can never know the kind of loneliness a woman knows. Man lies in a woman's womb only to gather strength, he nourishes himself from this fusion, and then he rises and goes into the world, into his work, into battle, into art. He is not lonely. He is busy. The memory of the swim in amniotic fluid gives him energy. The woman may be busy too, but she feels empty. Sensuality for her is not only a wave of pleasure in

* The calculated, however, are perhaps the most readily distinguishable of all masculine and feminine texts. The intellectual descent is like a descent into separate animal forms in which the two sexes (like hyenas and coyotes) give off rank, but separate, odors of mawkishness.

† Anaïs Nin, *Diary* (New York, Harcourt, Brace & World, 1966), Vol. I, pp. 184 and 190.

which she has bathed, and a charge of electric joy at contact with another. When man lies in her womb she is fulfilled, each act of love is a taking of man within her, an act of birth and rebirth, of child-bearing and man-bearing.*

The confusion of pregnancy and copulation is tasteless. Men enter vaginas, not wombs. And once born, they never "swim" again in amniotic fluid. But everything is too swimming here. Why is sensuality always a *wave* of pleasure in which one *bathes*? A particularly foolhardy immersion in view of that "charge of electric joy," a wonder that any human being comes out of bed alive. As for the basic contrast, men have not demonstrably shown less comprehension of loneliness than women. If women can be busy and feel empty, no doubt men can be busy and feel lonely. Dante rose and went into *The Divine Comedy* and *still* missed his own city. But the contrast is characteristic. As the writer recites the efficacy of male pursuits, she holds up a sign: *Women feel more generously, women feel more delicately*. It is like Megan Terry's handy appropriation of another shibboleth—in remarking about her own play, *Viet Rock*, "I think I'm, well, juicier than Brecht." †

Another effective, though less predictable, observation:

> Women are so much more honest than men. . . . A woman says, "I am jealous." A man covers it up with a system of philosophy, a book of literary criticism, a study of psychology.

* *Ibid.*, p. 106.
† Eleanore Lester, "At Yale: Joy, Baby, Joy," *New York Times*, October 9, 1966, Section 2, p. 1.

Henry [Miller] is so often confused, irrational, formless, like
D. H. Lawrence.*

In less rarefied circles than Miss Nin's, the question is
"Which sex is the more *dis*honest?" and women are generally supposed to be the answer. Probably no group of
people, steadily scrutinized by another, can afford to be
open. Such people (employees, Negroes, women) are driven
to subtlety, a sanctuary from examination. Perhaps only
those who hope to get their way by forthright statements
are determined to make them: all but the least vulnerable
feint, hide, circumlocute. And among animals, even these
merely *play* at courage. Having no bias against cowardice,
animals attack out of desperate rather than chivalric need,
and then only with some certainty of winning. To make
their purposes clear is a chore rather than an ideal.

Miss Nin herself wearies occasionally of her exquisite
chores, "Am I only a medium of clarity and harmony
through which others find themselves . . ." † and also

* Anaïs Nin, *Diary*, Vol. I, p. 240. Three feminine stereotypes (*confused, irrational* and *formless*) are transferred here to the men, whereupon the woman is relieved of them.

Miss Nin's incapacity for finding herself rather than her surroundings
at fault was perhaps a familial trait. Staying in a French hotel with her
father, Miss Nin left the bath water (which ran too slowly) running.
At breakfast below, the Nins saw the bath water running (briskly now)
down the main staircase. Joaquin Nin, on this account, wrote in the
"Livre d'Or" of the hotel: "This place is full of shit." But in fact, when
the Nins left it, the hotel was not full of shit, it was full of Miss Nin's
bath water.
† *Ibid.*, p. 143.

wearies of listening to Henry Miller. A reasonable fatigue, explained unreasonably:

> There are moments in Henry's talk when I feel truly tired, like a woman reaching for knowledge beyond her capacity. I stretch my mind to follow the curves and sweeps of man's mind. It is always the big, impersonal spaces which frighten me, the vast deserts, universe, cosmologies. How small my guiding lantern, how vast man's universe. It seems to me that what I hang onto is the human, and personal. I do not want to enter impersonal, non-human worlds.*

The passage capitalizes routinely upon our common distaste, in ignorance, for abstract knowledge. As in Rebecca West's description of "lunacy," impersonal thought and masculinity are simultaneously disparaged. Both writers, at their very different rates of metabolism, store up the same warm-human-glowing advantages of women.

The risks of imposed ideals are double: the temptation is to manifest them personally, like Miss Nin, or to urge them upon others. Both are sexual imitations—the first of faith, the second of its propagation. Willa Cather, for example, produced a vigorous, virile statement about women, affixing to them a species of conduct which men are believed to admire. Her Nebraskan wives bear large families in poverty; but even as they perform these duties (which, after all, women of many regions and temperaments perform), they

* *Ibid.*, p. 158.

are remarkably free of the sexual failings so often observed to be the concomitants of their sexual virtues. These women are stolid, muscular, even-tempered (laconic or jolly, but not moody) creatures, ideal men-in-women. Antonía wears men's clothes and conducts her first pregnancy and delivery as a Roman general would—or as he would suppose he would if, by mischance, he had to.

The only, but meaningful, drawback: Antonía's later and innumerable feats of reproduction amount to parthenogenesis. Her husband's part in her career, while polite, seems singularly small. It eventually emerges in these novels that Willa Cather's women consume their worlds: the company of men is socially tolerable, but so is their absence. The most admired of men, like Claude Wheeler in *One of Ours*, aspire to be feminine in spirit too, or are content, like Fred Ottenburg, to carry wardrobe trunks for such abstractions of talent as Thea Kronborg in *The Song of the Lark*.

George Eliot's dealing with this same issue, the possible conversion of the woman novelist to the dominant sexual ethic, is more interesting. Her original intention in *Middlemarch* seems to have been almost suffragette, directly to resent the confinement of feminine intelligence. A generalization, for example, about "modes of education which make a woman's knowledge another name for motley ignorance" appears in the first edition and later disappears. But still, in fact, nothing is more essential to the final book (the first image of the whole which always re-enters the mind) than Dorothea Casaubon's tardy comprehension of her husband's mind. This is the novel's instant of irreversible dismay, like the cracking open of an old egg. Untrained clarity confronts professional moribundity, it recognizes the futility of a life's work. The prospect, then, of conjoined waste has a selfish terror about it, the first frantic sense of a cheat. But the novel resumes—to equate Casaubon and connubial duty, to translate the intelligence of his wife into a "self-forgetful ardour." The Casaubon branch of the book becomes an apotheosis of Dorothea. She is pampered as the prettiest in a long, long procession of girl martyrs to matrimony.

But the issue revives, insidiously, in the alternate relations of the Lydgates. Before her marriage to Casaubon, Dorothea's encounters with Lydgate steadily implied the possibility of an ideal marriage with him—the suggestion that the two of them, like a piece of Soviet sculpture, might march forward (thick limbs entwined) in love, knowledge and industry. The Soviet suggestion is, in fact, a first element of the novel's subtle hostility toward Lydgate, who takes the suggestion too late and who dares, until then, to suppose he prefers to marry Rosamund Vincy.

A kind of revenge of Dorothea Casaubon's waste is taken through Lydgate's waste as well.* Obstensibly, he is praised

---

* It is not surprising that critics, such as Edward Dowden, have particularly objected to George Eliot's representation of Lydgate's failure. Walter Houghton attributes this objection to the intense value placed by Victorian critics upon optimism. (*The Victorian Frame of Mind*, pp. 302–03.) An uneasy sense of *Middlemarch*'s sexual hostility, however, may also have been involved. Certainly, Yeats's comment in *Ideas of Good and Evil* is a sexual rebuke: "George Eliot had a fierceness hardly

193

for his philanthropic intentions and pitied for the frustration of his abilities which his marriage brings about. And yet whenever he commands his wife, whenever he asserts the husband's authority (which Dorothea Casaubon has sublimely acknowledged), Rosamund flouts his control. Like a young, petticoated Casaubon, she too succeeds in remaining "a being apart." Her stupid "impassibility" is stronger than any intelligent direction of her conduct which Lydgate can devise. Rosamund is the demoniac center of the book, the worst (as Dorothea is presumably the best) which the subordinated can make of their subordination. The novelist deplores Rosamund's responses and yet takes a small, bitter pleasure in her mulish self-sufficiency, as in her gradual domination of a man who set off blithely in his preference for what he thought to be her naive adoration of his talents. Rosamund becomes the phlegmatic mistress, Lydgate the distraught servant.

The other women of the book are fragments split off, centrifugally, from the first source of the novel's energy. Mary Garth is a simple escape of self-sympathy: a girl (like the novelist) who is not indisputably beautiful, but clever and clear. Mrs. Garth has the usual concern of cardinals for the humility of curates. Resentment of her doctrine seeps down in the novel to the smallest Garth level—to the children Letty and Ben, who learn how each is different from the other under Mrs. Garth's reiterated suppression of Letty.

---

to be found but in a woman turned argumentative." And more recent masculine defences of even Casaubon's abilities, seem prompted by the same motive of sexual retaliation.

The older women of the book, Mrs. Cadwallader and Mrs. Farebrother, seem to have graduated from nubility and inhibition on the same day. Their age permits them to be bold, bossy, articulate—but their license to practice scarcely matters. The absorption of the book is in varieties of heterosexual compromise.

To concur with prevailing sexual opinions, even to George Eliot's extent—which was hardly more than to dramatize their difficulty—has since, in the best writing by women, grown obsolete. It is not that the opinions themselves have lost the attention, however reluctant, of those whom they describe. But the intellectual accommodation of these opinions, even in *Middlemarch*'s involuted mode, is no longer possible.

George Eliot's anger seems fortified by her objectivity, i.e., by her translation of the issue into "character" and "plot." When the novelist's concern shifts to self-examination, anger subsides into depression. Alex Comfort has recently argued, in *The Nature of Human Nature*, the right of the twentieth century to optimism: whatever have been the hideous events of the century, its people are still better off than people have ever been before. It is of course proper to discuss how people should feel, though the necessity of discussion must in itself prove that they feel somewhat differently. Most fictional reactions to the present century, whatever its superiority to the one before, suggest a new, an almost inventive or ingenious, sadness. This is shared, even intensified, by modern women writers who have chosen, seriously and directly, to describe their own experience. Isolating themselves as topics of the imagination, they seem to multiply their old actual (or social) isolation. Whatever their historical advantages over Charlotte Brontë or Mary Wollstonecraft, they lack the old verve—that fine pink-cheeked defiance with which the earlier women aired their minds.

Perhaps the change is explained by Mary Wollstonecraft's being one of the first to speak, and so being confident of others' listening. An entire sex, in the nineteenth century, seems to have had a fresh sense of being heard, much as an individual writer (in any period) has it at the beginning of his work. It does not seem possible then that one may be speaking only to himself. But that realization, particularly when their subject is also women, is palpable in modern women novelists. Beginning with Dorothy Richardson, the discontent with feminine stereotypes is not radically different from George Eliot's: what is different is the mode of expressing the dissociation. The newer impulse has been to discard preconception or prohibition by resorting to introspection alone. And it does not seem accidental that of the three writers who created the introspective, or psychological, novel, a woman (Dorothy Richardson) accompanies two men (Proust and Joyce) who are markedly indifferent to our customary heterosexual competitions in power.*

* It is true that in conversation Joyce repeated, like discoveries, the most hackneyed criticisms of women: "Women write books and paint pictures and compose and perform music. And there are some who have attained eminence in the field of scientific research. . . . But you have

In the United States, however, where behavior seems commonly more vocal, impatient and gregarious, feminine subjectivity has tended to be complicated by other and contrary states of mind—contrary, that is, to the utmost consistency of inwardness. Perhaps it is still our relative (national) youth—that those diversions from self-interest which obtained in the Victorian novel, particularly the diversion of company, have obtained longer in this country. In Edith Wharton, for example, social mores and individual responses assert equal and generally irreconcilable claims. And even if Edith Wharton's concern had been entirely individual, she did not have an innovative method, like Dorothy Richardson's, by which the concern might permeate the novel. At the same time, a valuable coarseness, a rude incapacity to be precious, works against subjectivity in an American like Mary McCarthy: so she would prefer, as she says, to be our (rather more emphatic) Jane Austen than ever our Virginia Woolf. Similarly, in Sylvia Plath's one short novel, *The Bell Jar*, and in Jane Bowles' *Two Serious Ladies*, a more grotesque (than satiric) wit offsets submergence in sensibility. By nature, wit seems to involve others; the self is seldom able to amuse the self.

But within the strict limits of this fictional response, which

---

never heard of a woman who was the author of a complete philosophic system, and I don't think you ever will." (Richard Ellmann, *James Joyce*, p. 648.)

But in his writing, though he touches on old stereotypes and establishes new ones (see p. 75), he reclaims them by affection, subtlety and wit. It is as though, arriving in heaven, one found that cats and crocodiles have immortal souls after all.

might be called a legitimate and chosen self-study, one feels nonetheless an incursion of that arid narcissism imposed by society. There is, for example, Doris Lessing's *Children of Violence*: the probable truths of this feminine history might almost as well be probable untruths, the effect of tedium is often so predominant:

> Martha was resentful; or rather, a small critical nerve in Martha was struck unpleasantly.

> Martha was alone in her room. She felt exposed, unable to bear other people.

> She could not help a pang of repulsion for the idea of an ulcer.

> She entered sleep cautiously, like an enemy country.*

How we *know* these sentences! The slowly grinding depression of the girl, all that lonely, anxious dissatisfaction, are now no more communicable than predictable. Even the girl's name, Martha *Quest*: no other psychic term has become so immediately numbing as the search-for-identity. It is not, of course, Doris Lessing's fault that a flock has fabricated what she attempted genuinely, that introspection can be (and has been) vulgarized as easily as, say, sexuality in the novel. And *Children of Violence* retains its own quality of implacable, even heroic, thoroughness. But still, its whole intention seems to have driven the writer toward the dulling of her own

* *Martha Quest*, pp. 114 and 206; *A Proper Marriage*, pp. 289 and 290, in *Children of Violence* (New York, Simon and Schuster, 1964).

talent. It is perhaps for this reason that she seems released into the space, however troubled, of the *African Stories*, into the social comedy of *In Pursuit of the English*, into the formal experimentation of *The Golden Notebook*.

In *Children of Violence* it is as though, having rejected the dramatic argument of *Middlemarch*, the woman novelist remains nonetheless under a compulsion to "answer" or at least mull over the same oppressive questions. The submergence into self is then perhaps no less retaliatory than George Eliot's openness—merely a modern mode of retaliation, comparable to the molluscan responses, for the Negroes, of the Black Muslim movement; for the young, of the hippie movement. The sense of sealing-off is the same. This quality attaches, of course, to the entire post-Freudian mode of fiction, but with particular fastness to its practice by the less secure castes. They seem no more solitary than shut out. They do not so much create their alienation, in the sense in which Camus and Sartre were free to create theirs, as attempt to accommodate an alienation (like a canopied bed or a grand piano) which they have been obliged to inherit. For women writers, as for Negro, what others have said bears down on whatever they can say themselves.* Both are like people looking for their own bodies under razed buildings, having to clear away debris. In their every effort to

---

* To this point, Ralph Ellison: "But when we Negro Americans start 'writing,' we lose this wonderful capacity for abstracting and enlarging life. Instead we ask, 'How do we fit into the sociological terminology? Gunnar Myrdal said this experience means thus and so. And Dr. Kenneth Clark, or Dr. E. Franklin Frazier, says the same thing. . . .' " ("An Interview with Ralph Ellison," *Harper's*, April 1967, p. 90.)

formulate a new point of view, one feels the refutation of previous points of view—a weight which must impede spontaneity. The primary impression of such work tends to be one of conscience, a reputable but hardly exhilarating faculty.

Women's books of this sort are tired forms of decision. If one thinks of the novel as an alternation, like labor and leisure, of decision and indecision, the first is direct, preferential, argumentative, even litigious. The basic activity is the separation of the admirable from the unadmirable. Beneath variously familiar psychological surfaces—say, Malamud's bumbling shabby fellows or Mailer's sweating and swearing ones—the work wears on: deciding for and against, for and against. The characters, whatever their postures of melancholy or effervescence, stand in a queue waiting to be passed or failed. Actual life appears to be supersaturated—suspending too much from judgment, holding too much in solution. The novelist's function is to bring some solids out of solution. His duty is to move events toward a point at which he may feel all about him, like cultivated fields stretching to the horizon, the impress of evaluation. The motive is, as Freud phrased it, to *put one's stamp* upon what has not shown this stamp before—or, as Norman Mailer has said, to bring about change.

Indecision may also involve the expression of innumerable opinions, judgments, distinctions. But these now cease to be vital to one's sense of the novel. On the contrary, it will seem light, particularized, neutral, without appetite for either stamp or change—and so, almost inevitably, static. The conclusion to which the novel comes will seem accidental rather than willed. Whatever the answer may be, it will seem less relevant than the entry into a question—rather as being alive underlies all conceivable solutions of living problems.

The highest ability to define a static condition need not, of course, eliminate the purpose of deciding upon it. The uncommitted young woman, for example, is a fixed and permanent image in Tolstoy, as much as in Jane Austen or in Wilde's *The Importance of Being Earnest*. Tolstoy could almost totally submerge his future (moral decision) in his present (sheer manifestation).* But still, *War and Peace* is a perfectly detailed brief. Tolstoy is distinct from Wilde and from Jane Austen in his relish of change and effect (which they avoid), and his zest is unmistakable in the presentation of the *altered* Natasha: fertile, industrious, running to fat, tamed. As in *Resurrection*, where all is moral proof, summary overwhelms particulars.

This kind of narrowing to the case has, since Tolstoy, increased—even as fatigue with it has increased. Argu-

---

* Immediately after speaking of Tolstoy's "amazing intellectual power," Virginia Woolf remarks: "There is in the work of the great classical writers a *finality* of effect which places certain of their scenes, apart from the story, *beyond the reach of change*. We do not ask what bearing they have upon the narrative, nor do we make use of them to interpret problems which lie on the outskirts of the scene. A laugh, a blush, half a dozen words of dialogue, and it is enough. . . ." [My italics.] (*Collected Essays*, New York, Harcourt, Brace & World, 1967, Vol. I, p. 262.)

mentative sexuality is now perhaps the first means, like a birthmark, of identifying American novels. At the same time, Tolstoy's immense curiosity, his faculty for becoming as much as judging the other, is presently rare. It is felt in Sartre, for whom the other has the fascination of an anagram, and in Joyce. One thinks of Norman Mailer's ideal of the woman's searching for the "best possible mate" and proceeding to "improve the species"—and then of Molly Bloom's inconsequence, "As well him as another." Joyce suggests that there is no form which the species can take which is not, at some moment, acceptable. Partners need only be alive at the same time. Mailer's emphasis falls upon preference, electing some and defeating others. He seems concerned with profitable investment in one of the few human actions, sexual choice, which still remains comparatively free of ambition, incautious and spendthrift. Though Mailer is the later writer and presumably the sexual revolutionist, it is in him, not in Joyce, that one finds an insistent sexual discrimination.

What is wearisome is the hunger for sexual opinion, decision, regulation. From time to time, it shifts effortlessly from women to male homosexuals—as though even those who are ravenous must occasionally vary their diet. An early example of the intellectual mastication involved: a decision against homosexuality made by the Oregon Supreme Court about fifty years ago. The attempt is the (by now) familiar one of assisting nature in the definition of the body's laws:

In the order of nature the nourishment of the human body is accomplished by the operation of the alimentary canal, beginning with the mouth and ending with the rectum. In this process food enters the first opening, the mouth, and residuum and waste are discharged through the nether opening of the rectum. The natural functions of the organs for the reproduction of the species are entirely different from those of the nutritive system. It is self-evident that the use of either opening of the alimentary canal for the purpose of sexual copulation is against the natural design of the human body. In other words, it is an offense against nature.*

Punctiliously observed, the law would eliminate kissing, since the mouth, as a nutritive entry, must be perverted by kissing (if not by *speech*) as well as by fellatio. The penis too becomes creation's misdemeanor, since its duality clearly violates the Oregon separation between digestive and sexual discharges. Copulation then must logically become another "offense against nature," just as it is the only animal means of continuing to be a part of nature.

A hubristic instance, obviously, and yet one recognizes in it the characteristic drive toward the efficient organization, the profitable arrangement, of sexual experience. It is only in degree, not in kind, different from Freud's intentions toward Martha Bernays:

I want to strengthen myself through you and then with renewed strength go on trying to improve my position. . . .†

* This decision was quoted by Jack Leavitt in his review of Bryan Magee's *One in Twenty* (*The Nation*, January 9, 1967, p. 54.)
† *The Letters of Sigmund Freud*, p. 113.

Or from Camus's entry in his *Notebooks*:

Sex leads to nothing. It is not immoral but it is unproductive. One can indulge in it so long as one does not want to produce. But only chastity is linked to a personal progress.*

It does not really matter that the two contradict each other. They are brothers under the time or place, in the sense that, whatever relationships they define between sexuality and progress, they are compelled to define them. The engrained conviction is that the person must make something, or make something of himself (again, no doubt, by making something), and that he does so by deciding the manner in which he should regulate what Dorothy Richardson, from an opposite persuasion, called "the worldwide everything." This "personal progress" is, of course, determinedly lofty—a *spiritual* progress, as we always say, applying our economy to heaven. But since the same procedures of forecast, estimate, selection and accumulation of credits are involved, it seems still a heaven for stockbrokers.

One might take as another instance of this predisposition, an event described in Lawrance Thompson's biography of Robert Frost—the death of Frost's first child, Elliott, at the age of four.† To enhance their grief, the parents were divided in their opinions of the death. It was Frost who discerned its moral meaning: he was being punished by the

* Albert Camus, *Notebooks, 1942–1951*, p. 36.
† Lawrance Thompson, *Robert Frost: The Early Years, 1874–1915* (New York, Holt, Rinehart and Winston, 1966), p. 258.

child's death for his neglect of the child. His wife found the death inexplicable, grief was meaningless to her. It was grief, the loss of a child was a loss. She resented in her husband's analysis the same vulgarity which Camus expresses, the same head for (moral) business. For if the child's death was to punish Frost, then he might "learn" by his punishment, he might be finally "a better person" for having suffered it. He would have made "personal progress." The rapidity with which Frost entered the death in his own moral accounts marks the decisive temper by which we are dominated.

And with which we are surfeited. Carlyle, hearing from Emerson that Margaret Fuller had agreed to accept the universe, pounded out, "By God, she'd better!" But now our minds work against Carlyle in the anecdote. Why should Margaret Fuller accept the universe? And why should Carlyle insist upon her doing so? His own acquiescence is less humble than irritable: his phrasing is out of that exhausted idiom of Victorian husbands, thundering over burnt porridge and unpaid bills. The "better" is indicative too, again of profitable ends. That which is firmly entrenched (a crime syndicate, say, or a universe) can be turned to more profit by seeming collusion than by detachment. The exterminator cannot pretend there are no starlings. He must want starlings to exist in order to advertise his lethal opinion of them. Like a novelist, he will study their intimate habits, become in imagination almost a starling himself, in order to decide more effectively against them. One might say, crazily, "There is no Asia" or "I do not accept Asia." Such statements would not fall within the decisive mode.

Within that mode, one studies Asia, one becomes almost Asian (like a CIA agent disguised as a coolie), in order to decide against Asia, to recommend that the East henceforward model itself upon the West.

Both sexes, of course, can alternate between both points of view. Though, historically, men have been judges more often than women, and women prostitutes more often than men, neither point of view can be considered sexually predestined. It is Joyce in Dublin, for example, who chose "silence, exile and cunning," all conventional attributes of the defendant or the woman.* Similarly, on the topic of women's clothes, Rousseau and Mary Wollstonecraft seemed to exchange customary sexual postures. In *Emile*, Rousseau comments upon a woman's appropriate dress:

> Her dress is extremely modest in appearance, and yet very coquettish in fact: she does not make a display of her charms, she conceals them; but in concealing them, she knows how to affect your admiration. Everyone who sees her will say, There is a modest and discreet girl; but while you are near her, your eyes and affections wander all over her person, so that you cannot withdraw them; and you would conclude, that every part of her dress, simple as it seems, was only put in its proper order to be taken to pieces by the imagination.

This could be posted on Balenciaga's front door, as a proclamation of Sophisticated Dress. But Mary Wollstonecraft

---

* These are precisely the techniques, for example, of Jane Austen's *Mansfield Park*, the means by which Fanny Price, for all her rather aggressive probity, saves herself. Submitted to emotional exile, she *exerts* silence and, in the narrow sense of knowing how to wait, cunning.

is outraged: "Is this modesty? Is this a preparation for immortality?" * The notion that every dress should prepare every woman for immortality seems out of the Oregon Supreme Court mind; one is reminded of the fundamental grimness with which Norman Mailer thinks of every pickle or ice-cream cone as an index of intestinal morality.

It is not surprising that the French are thought, in comparison to either Englishmen or Englishwomen (or to Americans), to be effeminate, i.e., sexually subtle and guileful. Flaubert said of Emma Bovary, "C'est moi," and though he precedes George Eliot (and is imitated by her†), he is "later" in his recommendation to novelists, "Ne pas conclure." He seems detached from the legislative mode which still prevails, in all but his feeling that he too must *conclude* not to conclude. At the same time (as national stereotypes are dubious as well), France is capable of producing its own Mary Wollstonecraft. For example, in Simone de Beauvoir's *Memoirs of a Dutiful Daughter,* an account of the writer's bursting through family restrictions, one easily recognizes the familiar conception of the self: the supreme right of self-realization, the sententious refusal of claims which threaten to inhibit the self's *progress*—a progress which is not less doctrinaire than Freud's or Camus's because, in Simone de Beauvoir's case, it is feminine. In fact, the fear of similarity

* Mary Wollstonecraft, *The Rights of Woman* (London, Everyman's Library, 1955), p. 97

† In *Middlemarch,* Rosamund Lydgate's ill-fated decision, against her husband's wishes, to go horseback-riding with her brother-in-law, is a discreet echo of Emma Bovary's riding with Rodolphe. The one expedition brings about Rosamund's miscarriage; the other, Emma's adultery.

rather than of emulation may account for the particularly fierce dislike which men express for primarily decisive women writers like Beauvoir. It is Susan Sontag's impression that these critics are jealous of their sexual monopoly of the riding crop.* But, in their (shall we say) defense, it seems possible that they are naturally dismayed by the prospect of everyone's wanting to hurt, by the potential of tedium. In the happiest of worlds, they presuppose matching and cooperative pleasures: some who enjoy whipping, others who enjoy being whipped. If anything, at the moment, innovation in the novel consists of a preference for *apparently* beaten or self-beaten men. But it is not so easy to shake a habit: underneath the dandruff and the wrinkles, the same old senators and representatives are gesturing emphatically. A more profound reaction, of deliberate and retaliatory frivolity, is evident in new forms of music and art.

If fish considered anything, they would consider sexual rivalry as preposterous as we would consider rivalry in defecation. (Though, of course, even this idea is not remote for us—small boys compete in urination and "great-bladdered Emer," Cuchulain's wife, was renowned throughout Ireland.) But on land, where reproduction depends upon internal fertilization, the lower male animals must inevitably experience anxiety, rivalry, responsibility. To save themselves repeated injury, they resort to hierarchical order. A

* Carolyn C. Heilbrun, "Speaking of Susan Sontag," *New York Times Book Review*, August 27, 1967, p. 30.

few male sage grouse assume the ranks of lieutenant grouse
and sergeant grouse. Each two officers command seven
grouse privates, who function only as guards on the perim-
eter of the mating area, like eunuchs at court. The females
wait in the center, where the natural style is cool, seemingly
indifferent and irresponsible. In some species, irresponsibility
mounts to a crazy gayety. One female insect is prone to
sudden flight during sexual engagement, in mischievous dis-
regard of the male whose mating position is awkward, managed only by extreme contortion. Such responses must not
abate the male impression, on every sensate level, of sexual
life as a sober, desperate and even treacherous undertaking,
and May flies might endorse Goethe's glum remark: "How
dare a man have a sense of humor when he considers his
immense burden of responsibilities toward himself and
others. . . ." *

We assume that authority and responsibility are incompatible with amusement. Ralph Ellison has described the
Southern white's sense of the unattainable pleasures of the
Southern Negro's Saturday night. By whatever accident control is placed in one human group, another will assume the
characteristics of contradiction. In this way, women too have
been repeatedly allied to frivolity, improvidence, guile and
disobedience—which must survive as stubbornly as their
counters of solemnity, forthrightness and instruction. Not
surprisingly, then, it is under this same guise that women
have most often written effectively—under the guise too of

* Quoted by W. H. Auden in "Mr. G.," *New York Review of Books,*
February 9, 1967, p. 10.

strategy and wile. They have little historical reason to share that hatred of "craft," for example, which amounts in some other writers to an identification of artifice with degeneracy. It becomes essential then for the novelist to protest his haste and immediacy, to preserve an edge of disarray like a badge of honor. To be truthful, the talent must not seem premeditated, aforethought (the law repeats the same preference of impulse to contrivance)—above all else, it must seem rude, rough, contemptuous of practiced skill. But the opposite inclination is to place everything in the skillful arrangement of words, making them a barrier to impulse. In Ivy Compton-Burnett's novels, words are like mummies, embalmed and motionless.

It is possible, for nonfighters, neither to referee nor to take fighting seriously. In the late summer, in the Rome zoo, even the polar bears eat enormous quantities of tomatoes. A writer can seem to run with the crowd, and actually slow it by indicating its ridiculous single-mindedness. But this is a rare frivolity, depending upon a rare combination of faculties: not only talent and certainly not only sex, but an indiscriminate attachment as much to the unballasted as to the steady. Pope is among the few who have realized the potential beauty of mindlessness: a human condition like mindfulness, and, in *The Rape of the Lock*, just as instinct with attraction. To encounter Sterne's Uncle Toby or Jane Austen's Mr. Woodhouse is to learn that inanity is priceless. Why do we remember with primary (if silent) pleasure Mr. Woodhouse's foolish adoration of his daughter, when what we emphasize, in discussing the book, are Emma's defects and their proper correction? Through our habit of judgment, we insist upon the opposite of what we have enjoyed the most, i.e., the *absence* of judgment in the relations of Emma and her father. Nothing, as long as they are together, need ever change or improve in either of them. An attachment to aim or improvement, in fact, impairs their variety of comic stasis. George Eliot cannot give her Mr. Brooke in *Middlemarch* an equal autonomy, her purposefulness is too abrasive. Just as her ambition would undoubtedly dismiss Pope's Belinda too harshly—as still another of those "elegant-minded canary birds" whom she despised.

Of course, the circumstances of Jane Austen's society reinforced her frivolity. These circumstances are now, for us, irrecoverable and undesirable as well: I am thinking of the unmitigated leisure of both sexes in the one class which Jane Austen studied. And this leisure combined easily with a class contempt for "trade" and even for the now reputable professions of law and medicine.* A gentleman of her society would as soon be a rosebush as a surgeon, and Jane Austen herself would be incapable of the hymn to dentistry which appears, a hundred years later, in Dorothy Richardson's *Pilgrimage*. But it is pointless to repeat our egalitarian complaints. The social organization which Jane Austen accepts,

---

* It is true that in *Mansfield Park*, the clergyman is disparaged only by Mary Crawford, whose moral sensibility is known to be coarsened. And when at last he hears his call, the Rev. Edmund Bertram is taken much more seriously than Mr. Collins is in *Pride and Prejudice*. It is interesting, though, that some readers have felt Jane Austen failed even this profession, that her account of it in *Mansfield Park* is painfully deficient in holiness.

almost entirely relieves her of that sexual solemnity which, especially in the United States, is closely involved with an awe of exertion, work, aggression against odds—an ethic of enterprise.

Jane Austen, on the contrary, had available to her imagination a scene which must now seem to us singularly monistic: neither sex appears to be good or bad for much. The lives of her characters never generate a consequence sufficient to weight them down. The men and women are alike, virtually one, in dealing with little and affecting even less. Hence, their misconceptions of themselves—their heady sensations of efficacy or righteousness or authority—become their comic assets. Their costuming themselves in means, as they are politely conducted toward their ends, cannot disguise their fundamental helplessness. It is an *antic* helplessness, since it need not distress them—not deeply, at any rate. After all, their sheer existence will help them to their wants —no great effort on its part, either, since the wants, like the wanters, are smaller than they, the wanters, think—or to substitutes which prove to be as gratifying as the original choices. Living in an "ocean of air," the characters drift about and, eventually, encounter each other. These encounters are wrapped for them in expressions of will and purpose. The dialogue is dancelike, the weaving partners are assertion and actuality, will and being, moving to the rhythms of self-incomprehension.

There is no ethical sweep. If one reads Jane Austen, as Charlotte Brontë did, for the definition of ideals rather than of delusions, he is bound to be disappointed. In fact, most criticism of her displays either such disappointment or mis-placed gratification, i.e., an insistence upon the sober significance of her work. If it has none, it will still be found to have at least some. But both readings, resentful and laborious, are directed by the same anticomic prejudgment which Charlotte Brontë first expressed with all due ardor. Central to this point of view, which still predominates in our own fiction, are (1) the importance of self-determination, (2) the importance of effort and resistance, and, in preparation for this variety of experience, (3) the importance of analyzing one's resources, distributing them according to their proper employments. The last furnishes the dualism which is absent in Jane Austen, and ever-present in Charlotte Brontë.

What seems rebellious in Charlotte Brontë, then, is instead imitative, the appropriation of a modest and utilitarian Byronism by the woman writer. Quite consistently, Matthew Arnold objected to *Villette* in exactly the terms he might have objected to Byron's *Manfred:* "the writer's mind contains nothing but hunger, rebellion, and rage." * Conventionally, all degrees of personal clamor receive attention as "rebellions," a fixation which overlooks the essential anarchy of detachment. It must always be assumed too that passion is honesty, that to feel strenuously insures one's seeking the truth strenuously. Actually, for Charlotte Brontë, any indication that passion might be ineffectual or that will might be illusory aroused her hostility more quickly than her curiosity. The suggestion she took from Harriet Mar-

* *Letters,* Vol. I, p. 34. Quoted in Walter Houghton, *The Victorian Frame of Mind,* pp. 301–02.

tineau's and Henry Atkinson's *Laws of Man's Nature and Development*, that human beings might be only "circlings of force" (as, in fact, they appear in Jane Austen), prompted a preference for *not* learning, rather than learning, the anti-pathetic truth:

> Sincerely, for my own part I wish to find and know the Truth; but if this be Truth, well may she guard herself with mysteries, and cover herself with a veil.*

The triteness of the opinion and its inevitably falling into terms of prudery (everywhere one looked in 1841, a female body needed a veil) indicate the limits of this rebellion.

Its activities are those with which we are still familiar. The novelist performs autopsies, isolates separate organs, determines the hierarchy of their functions. There are endless distinctions: ideal and actual, spiritual and material, heart and mind, body and soul, hand and foot. One thinks of Jane Eyre's reaction against St. John Rivers' proposal of marriage:

> Can I receive from him the bridal ring, endure all the forms of love (which I doubt not he would scrupulously observe) and know that the spirit was quite absent? No: such a martyrdom would be monstrous.

Ah, the boldness, the clarity, the vigor of this consciousness. The decision with which "the spirit" of love is removed, like an appendix or a spleen, from the adjacent "forms" of love.

* Mrs. Gaskell, *Life of Charlotte Brontë*. Quoted in Walter Houghton, *The Victorian Frame of Mind*, p. 68.

214

But, in fact, Rivers' deplorable failure to distinguish between the two might have, in another novel, some viability:

> . . . Undoubtedly enough of love would follow upon marriage to render the union right even in your eyes.

Here he is damned for suggesting the promiscuous relations of body and soul to which Jane Austen could have assented. Though, at the same time, it is difficult to be sure which intensity, Rochester or Rivers, summer or winter, she would have found the more rashly immoderate. Not that the two minds are in total disagreement. Caution is not that much different from an eagerness to refuse. Once the free consciousness is challenged in *Jane Eyre* by sexual impropriety, it shifts into reserve. In this valley too, the dolls are delivered only upon receipt of a written contract. If anything, one is left after all the fuss with an even more acrid taste of the business, a retrogression from modest to wuthering self-interest.

Jane Austen codified experience less, if only by speaking of less. She had the negative virtue of keeping her mouth shut on a number of subjects. For example, we do not hear her on Shakespeare—an omission which, in view of the dramatic opinions expressed in *Mansfield Park*, must be considered happy. But we have Charlotte Brontë on Shakespeare—characteristically, in the course of directing someone else's reading:

> Now don't be startled at the names of Shakespeare and Byron. Both these were great men, and their works are like themselves.

You will know how to choose the good, and to avoid the evil; the finest passages are always the purest, the bad are invariably revolting; you will never wish to read them over twice. Omit the comedies of Shakespeare and the "Don Juan," perhaps the "Cain," of Byron, though the latter is a magnificent poem.*

Laugh, and choose evil. The Victorian association between levity and misconduct†—an association toward which Jane Austen was drawn only reluctantly and incompletely, since it must indict her own talent—compels the rejection of *Don Juan*. But our own taste in Byron (by which we in turn, perhaps, are helplessly directed) is closer to Jane Austen's. Instead of objecting to Byron's levity, she found it hard to respect his sobriety. Captain Benwick with Anne Elliott in *Persuasion:*

. . . Having talked of poetry, the richness of the present age, and gone through a brief comparison of opinion as to the first-rate poets, trying to ascertain whether *Marmion* or *The Lady of the Lake* were to be preferred, and how ranked the *Giaour* and *The Bride of Abydos*, and moreover, how the *Giaour* was to be pronounced, he shewed himself so intimately acquainted with all the tenderest songs of the one poet, and all the impassioned descriptions of hopeless agony of the other; he repeated, with such tremulous feeling, the various lines which imaged a broken heart, or a mind destroyed by wretchedness, and looked so entirely as if he meant to be understood, that

* Mrs. Gaskell, *Life of Charlotte Brontë.* Quoted in Walter Houghton, *The Victorian Frame of Mind*, p. 357.
† Walter Houghton, *The Victorian Frame of Mind*, pp. 300 and 356–58.

she ventured to hope that he did not always read only poetry; and to say, that she thought it was the misfortune of poetry, to be seldom safely enjoyed by those who enjoyed it completely; and that the strong feelings which alone could estimate it truly, were the very feelings which ought to taste it but sparingly.

A seemingly ladylike commentary, and yet ranging in its mockery: from the poetry of sensibility itself, to the conversational inanities it provokes and the individual poses it encourages. A particular sport is made of Charlotte Brontë's favorite autopsical divisions—broken *hearts* and wretched *minds* and tremulous *feelings*. How is there any knowing where Captain Benwick's spirit ends and his body starts? Like Jane Eyre, the Captain himself feels quite certain of his spirit's whereabouts and of its woeful condition. But beneath the sublimities of his evening chatter, Jane Austen indicates a daylight person, healthy and whole. Nothing is seriously wrong with the Captain: he experiences an understandable but hardly terminal discomfort. He enjoys Byron because he has lost a marriageable girl when he wanted to get married. He must be a lost spirit until, in the next chapter, his body meets another marriageable body. It might be more sensible of him not to parade his short-lived malaise —and Anne Elliott therefore teases, even as she indulges, him. But she acknowledges to herself that his plight is only an exaggeration of her own—an excessively open loss of the *sang-froid* which love diminishes in every lover.

217

Remoteness or mild negation, like a hand trailing in the water, alleviates purpose. Wherever commitment to codes of energy has been intense, the impulse to chafe at these codes—or rather, merely to suspend due observation of them—must be as natural as endorsement. The predilection of several women writers seems now, perhaps without their willing it to be, another and a new failure to accept the universe. A chillier matter than defiance, which sweats as much as defence; a Talmudic rather than Napoleonic disposition of the talent. Once in the Talmud, the blessings received by a prominent rabbi are debated. The first scholar says, The rabbi was blessed by not having a daughter. The second scholar says, The rabbi was blessed by having a daughter. Both statements are made with precision and seeming finality. Neither emerges as the truth. Not even fact emerges: did the rabbi have a daughter? Similarly, in the novel, formality may perversely heighten the sense of indulgence, of indecision within assertion. The scene in *Madame Bovary* which George Eliot remembered in *Middlemarch*, Emma's riding into the woods with Rodolphe, remains (emotionally, as the Talmudic debate remains intellectually) beyond decision. It is impossible ever to conclude *It was good* or *It was bad*. No later imitation of the scene (by George Eliot, by Willa Cather in *The Lost Lady*, by Philip Roth in the "Passion Paradise" bits of *When She Was Good*) is capable of that original exclusion of judgment.

This unfixed ambiance can easily accommodate itself to the appearance of opinions. In Ivy Compton-Burnett, definite "points of view" are repeatedly stated in asides intended to be overheard. But the fact that they are stated as asides sets them aside. They are not central, the situation remains intact beyond such comments upon it. If anything, its inaccessibility is heightened by these small glancing, tangential contacts. Dorothy Richardson was also capable, to a fault, of playing it discursive, prejudicial, emphatic—there is all that blithering about *men* and their supposed limitations and defects. And yet these exasperating little reproofs are like motes in the bright light air of *Pilgrimage*. Their infinitesimal weights bob up and down in its large mobility, contributing in the end to one's sense of the suspension of the mind in mindless being. The effect is finally uncommitted: one of these Richardson "opinions" was, in fact, that women should enter Parliament without joining parties and that they should join all churches (at least, in her mock-eclectic view, all the churches of Christendom).

The interest in phenomena is unlimited, the customary urge to categorize them is restrained. The novelist may, in this way, escape the necessity to be representative, of her sect or sex or era. If anything is accented, it can be eccentricity—as natural and ubiquitous as type. So a freedom can come about at least from pomposity, from the *we* bulging now inside the pseudo-*I*. The nineteenth-century novelist seems the archetypal *we*, but representation was then more modest, really, since it was frankly editorial. Now one thinks of the inane plurality of Lyndon Johnson's statement, *We are going to the hospital, we will have a polyp removed from our throat*—when what could be more personal and idiosyncratic than a polyp in a throat? Or of the lonely single man in Malamud's work, who is always and utterly, in fact, Man—virtuous, struggling, right and representative Man. Or, again, of Johnson's reputed mastery of the emotions, as he salutes Mrs. Johnson after dinner: "He enfolds her in his arms and says goodnight as he says everything else, with authority." * I should think the particular forte of some recent women novelists has been to recognize that the last thing a character can say with authority is *good night*, and that the less the novelist herself says with authority, the better.

Perhaps too, the less she says seriously. Without any great increment of social confidence, there has occurred nonetheless a marked disavowal of sobriety. And this seems to have been made possible through the disavowal, in turn, of estimation as "the point" of the novel. As long as one postulates that the novel must "make sense" of reality, he is committed to sobriety—for what sense except a sober sense (even if it sidles out, say, as "black humor") could be made of the reality we are furnished? But, obviously, it is equally possible to postulate senselessness, or the difficulty of separating what little sense there is from senselessness, or even the neglect inflicted upon this preponderant senselessness by an exclusive interest in sense. Then idiosyncrasies and even defects take on the interest previously or conventionally devoted to types—and may forestall the judgment, or even the definition, of types. In the old Jewish joke, the recognition of the type, The Friend, is endlessly delayed by

* Jim Bishop, *A Day in the Life of President Johnson* (New York, Random House, 1967), p. 269.

the recitation of his pimples, his wart, his hunchback, his harelip—and strangely, all of these malformations, remembered meticulously, become both empathetic and funny. As the drive toward recognition or identification is relinquished, the effect of leisure, even of inertia, sets in—one might speak of some recent novels simply as abstaining from speed. And with this inertia, the essential atmosphere of comedy is insured, a divorce from the reaching of conclusions. The sense develops of how much that is peculiar cannot and need not be altered. It is this playing over elements of static imperfection which coincides in Dickens' novels with a serious desire to bring about changes, but which entirely directs Chaucer in his dealing with the Prioress and the Wife of Bath. The equal receptivity there to both the precious and the coarse, like Jane Austen's equal receptivity to both intelligence and idiocy in *Emma*, is characteristic of the mode.

In novels now, however, which succeed to a long reign of consequence, it seems necessary to the reinstatement of the inconclusive, to be rid of the established form of the novel—with which Jane Austen was able to do nicely. There must be in the very arrangement of words an effect of exhilaration rather than of desperation, of purposelessness rather than of progress. In Mary McCarthy, this effect is confined to her repeated thesis that where progress has been supposed, there has actually been none; that most modern intellectual activity, with a great flexing of muscles and jaws, produces nothing that was not there before—"The Portrait of the Intellectual as a Yale Man," *The Oasis, The Groves of Academe.* But, in fact, Miss McCarthy argues this thesis of purposelessness with so much purpose of her own, that the novel itself is not in the least reconstituted. In *The Group*, of course, she considered the alternative of allowing the deluded to speak for themselves. But how palpable her own consciousness is within theirs! The young women seem constantly rebuked—even as they speak, they are spoken *to*, by their governess. It is not surprising that such a novelist should admit, with some irritation, to feeling inhibited by the novel and to preferring the autobiographical freedom of her *Memories of a Catholic Girlhood*. She is rather like Charlotte Brontë, desperate to speak out, to put her stamp (on reason now, instead of passion)—and yet a Charlotte Brontë who knows *Jane Eyre* has worn out.

This is the awkward position of a good many novelists now, from which only a few have extricated themselves: among women, especially Nathalie Sarraute and Ivy Compton-Burnett. What Charlotte Brontë disparaged as Jane Austen's velleities of the sewing room find their modern continuance in Nathalie Sarraute's "sub-conversations," as perhaps (a second channel crossing) Françoise Sagan descends from the Brontës. One recognizes in Sarraute the same removal from the major, the same fixing upon the minor and presumably irrelevant, the same qualification of the sufficiency of primary forces which is implied by dwelling upon secondary intricacies. Jane Austen's minutiae are liminal, Nathalie Sarraute's are subliminal, but they are alike in refusing to bypass detail. Neither is interested in the explicit speed of which the novel is capable, only in the nuances which must tend to delay it. In her own discussions of the

novel, Nathalie Sarraute is entirely antiprogressive. In criti-
cizing ordinary dialogue, she dislikes its haste: there not
being "time" for the person to consider a remark's ramifica-
tions, his having to speak and to listen frugally, his having
to rush ahead toward his object—which is of course "to
order his own conduct." * Her praise—for example, of
Proust—falls repeatedly upon the *minute*, the *slight*, the *tiny*.
Her search, which is more rewarded in Ivy Compton-Burnett
than in Proust, is always for the *numerous*, *secret* and *hidden*
elements, as for the veins of the hands which previously
waved or clapped in the novel. Her chief pleasure is taken
in the *taut* or *tense phrase*. For its sake, she entertains quite
happily the probability of *slackened* action or, as she finds
it in Ivy Compton-Burnett, perfunctory event.

Neither does she care about Ivy Compton-Burnett's resorting to narrative conventions, such as *said she* and *replied
he*, for which in other novelists she shows a most rigorous
contempt. The omnipresent "said Miss Burtenshaw" in *A
House and Its Head* makes no pretense of representing actual
speech. On the contrary, the insistence of these tags informs
us that this is not "life" at all, but artifical arrangement.
Anthony Burgess no doubt properly calls such a novel "sexless," since it refuses the first characteristic of sexual reality,
urgency. His own comedy, like Malamud's, runs on that
familiar track: urgency *frustrated*, desire *thwarted*—by impotence or change of mind or inopportunity. The techniques
of all the old fictional conflicts—between feeling and physi-

---

* Nathalie Sarraute, *The Age of Suspicion*, translated by Maria Jolas
(New York, Braziller, 1963), p. 105.

ology or feeling and thought or feeling and surroundings—
remain much the same. But in Ivy Compton-Burnett, a distance from urgency, from *nature* or *progress*, is maintained
by formal syntax.

In an interesting interview, Frank Kermode has presented
her with the generally known reservations about her novels:
don't all the characters talk alike? don't they lack (Dicken-
sian) differentiations by class, sex, age? She does not agree.
At any rate, the "normal," she says, is "keyed up," the plot
is "imposed." * Peculiarity no longer depends upon the accent of a Cockney or the accent of a BBC news announcer,
it is all-pervasive. *No* human beings talk the way these
characters do: in this sense, they all talk the same (un-
earthly) language. The entire method of actual communication is discarded. Words are used to imply, again, the raw
practical haste to which actual communication reduces people. Here words play undertow to the customary tide, the
forward pounding of realism is prevented by form. In Sylvia
Plath's *The Bell Jar*, metaphor acts as the protective barrier
between the novelist and the madness she deals with, at once
describing and confining its nature. So in Ivy Compton-
Burnett, speech separates the speaker from his feelings. Even
as he expresses them with an uncanny and impossible ac-

* Frank Kermode, "The House of Fiction," *Partisan Review*, Spring
1963, pp. 70–74.

Rather as modern painters will occasionally demonstrate that they can
"draw" (if they want to), Ivy Compton-Burnett will sometimes allow an
utterance to reflect the personality, education, etc., of a character. An
example is the nursemaid Marshall's letter in *A House and Its Head*.
Thomas Hardy could have been proud of it.

curacy, they seem to cease to be feelings, or *his* feelings; they become static and finished aspects of being alive, rather than the emotions which propel behavior.

For example, a character's restatement of an American conviction, "I think a life of individual effort is fully as dignified as one of inherited ease," is singularly unconvincing. The endorsement of exercise is lost in its stiff expression. So one suddenly sees effort as an unchanging aspect of existence. Similarly, in Jane Bowles' *Two Serious Ladies* the brief, formal, polite and noncommittal response to some ardent plea or remonstrance indicates not opposition so much as distance. Pleas and remonstrances, it is suggested, do not necessarily bring about *changes* in either the speaker or the person spoken to. They may be like showers of pebbles, after which an original silence resumes. But just as often, in Jane Bowles, those circumstances which ordinarily cause nothing, evoke no response—such as passing a stranger in the street—flower into situations. These, in turn, come to nothing in any dramatic sense: they seem merely, in themselves, unlikely, eccentric, curiously diverting.

This indication of idleness is more thoroughly verbal in Ivy Compton-Burnett. The choice of an infant's name, for example, ceases to be a problem when the problem is expressed on two levels of speech in succession:

"What is to be the designation of the youngest member of our community?" said Miss Burtenshaw.

"Yes, what is Baby's name?" said Mrs. Bode, content to speak according to herself.

225

A rare contentment in this context, for which Mrs. Bode rightly receives an elaborate commendation. Such exaggerated attention to the manner, rather than the import, of speech is common to all the characters. Like Oscar Wilde, Ivy Compton-Burnett repeatedly inserts the conventional remark in order to question it:

> "Well, appearances are deceitful," said Miss Burtenshaw, "or we must hope so."
> "Have we not a way of maligning appearances?" said Oscar. "They tend to be the expression of the truth."

> "Well, Nance," said Mrs. Bode, "I remember you the heroine of a like occasion, as if it were yesterday."
> "People who remember things, always remember them as if they were yesterday," said Cassie. "I remember it as if it were twenty-six years ago."

In the urgent mode, the phrases disputed here rush through en route to changes or conclusions or to new generalizations piled upon the old. But now a brake is kept on that kind of meaningfulness. "It is tiresome of exceptions to prove rules," a character remarks. The preference is to find no profitable use of exceptions, and to give entire attention to how exceptional they are. Few rules are proven and, perhaps consequently, few actions are taken:

> "I know you want me to go away."
> "You should suppress the knowledge, if you are not going to act upon it."

The simplest apprehension of motive is forestalled (suppressed) by the involuted and acidic response.

Ivy Compton-Burnett is of course capable of sudden aphoristic generalizations of her own:

"Dignity is always aimed at when circumstances preclude it."

"No friendship that is lost has ever been worth having."

But they are stationary and inutile within their frames—rather as infants, lying flat on their backs, furiously ride unseen bicycles. The extreme exactitude of the aphorism must always tend to impede progress—as Samuel Beckett's sentences, partly through their abstruse vocabulary, seem to resist continuation. One appears to follow another with reluctance, against inertia; or else a single sentence winds on confusedly, as though lost instead of going home.

It is a mode adapted to either sex's awareness of under-life, particularly in the sense of what merely passes without producing or achieving demonstrable effects. If it now proves to be a mode congenial to feminine talent, perhaps it is only that women have had ample historical opportunity to learn the under-life well. The shift is from significance to insignificance. The housewife who is bound and gagged by an armed robber furnishes a complete event: the victim confronts the aggressor, one is innocent and the other guilty, one evokes pity and the other resentment, one must be rescued (or mourned) and the other caught. Meanwhile, other housewives are moseying about their houses, inconclusively. The first subject is meant for Truman Capote, the second for Dorothy Richardson. It was she who first subsisted upon the intricacies of the not remarkable, the scarcely noticeable sequence of impressions which run between the hemorrhagic moments of drama. The common vaginal conception of women as dark and hidden sensibilities can be exploited by women writers, through their acknowledging that most experience is obscure, seemingly incomplete, responsive rather than efficient—Nathalie Sarraute's *tropismes*, the silent bendings and swayings of attitude, like reeds in water, beneath the surface of discourse.

"Women walking, women talking, women weeping!" said Duncan. "Doing all they can do. I will thank you to let me pass, as I am to catch a train this morning. Otherwise I would ask less. Your chatter may wait, as it is what the day holds for you."

So the novel, like Duncan and his female relatives (in *A House and Its Head*), may be seen as catching trains or staying at home, impatient or idle. And like these women talking, words relieved of reality become solely concerned with their appearance. Invariably, then, the obverse of intent proves to be nicety. An odd small company in English —Jane Austen, Oscar Wilde, Dorothy Richardson, Ivy Compton-Burnett, Jane Bowles—are linked by this effeminate precision. As, in the opposite mode, the torrential imprecision of Dickens is nonetheless congruous with, say, the laborious imprecision of Dreiser. In the first group, vivacity is more valued than drive, and complication than judgment.

The writer cares less for what is resolved by the dialogue than for the recognition, in its course, of all its conceivable diversions into related (or, for that matter, unrelated) issues. Oblivious of timetables, the speakers proceed (if that is quite the word) by reviving minor possibilities presumably long since denied—the possibility of a middle-class wife's happiness in the company of prostitutes in Jane Bowles' *Two Serious Ladies*, the legitimacy of cowardice in Ivy Compton-Burnett's *A House and Its Head*:

> "I think," said Cassie, "that it is best to let someone in a great difficulty get out of it in any way she has thought of. We hardly have a human right to prevent it. The remedy cannot be worse than the disease. We must leave her her own solution."

Once the rule of courage is suspended, admirable exceptions of cowardice are released.

Index